A SMALL BUSINESS GUIDE
TO EMPLOYEE SELECTION

A SMALL BUSINESS GUIDE TO EMPLOYEE SELECTION

Finding, interviewing, and hiring the right people

Lin Grensing

SELF-COUNSEL SERIES

International Self-Counsel Press Ltd.
Vancouver   Toronto

Self-Counsel Press Inc.
Seattle

Printed in Canada

Canadian Cataloguing in Publication Data

Grensing, Lin, 1959-
    A small business guide to employee selection

    (Self-counsel series)
    ISBN 0-88908-638-9

    1. Employee selection.   I. Title.   II. Series.
HF5549.5.S38G74 1986   658.3'112   C86-091435-6

Cover design by Sara Woodwark

SELF-COUNSEL SERIES

International Self-Counsel Press Ltd.
Editorial Office
306 West 25th Street
North Vancouver, British Columbia
V7N 2G1 Canada

Self-Counsel Press Inc.
1303 N. Northgate Way
Seattle, Washington 98113
U.S.A.
A subsidiary of International Self-Counsel Press Ltd.

CONTENTS

LIST OF SAMPLES

LIST OF TABLES

INTRODUCTION

So you're looking for a new employee. Perhaps your business is expanding faster than you expected and you need new staff, or you're having to replace a long-time valued employee who's retiring or moving away. It seems like a straightforward task upon first consideration.

But have you anticipated every possible problem? Have you thought through all the stages in the hiring process? Have you considered —

- Pre-hiring — what you need to do before you even begin
- Advertising effectively for job candidates
- Designing a workable application form
- Screening resumes to select the best candidates
- Conducting the interview
- Asking the right questions
- Asking sensitive questions
- Checking references
- Making your selection
- Orienting your new employee

When you need to hire, you need to do it in the most cost effective and time efficient manner possible. Are you confident that you'll be able to pick the best candidate from the many potential employees you'll have to consider?

In a survey conducted by the Thomas Magnum Company of Los Angeles, it was found that most companies spend between $10,000 and $30,000 to hire someone for an executive position. While hiring a clerical worker or laborer won't be quite as expensive, the costs will still be significant. Some of the tangible costs you will have include advertising, credit and reference checks, personnel

department overhead, telephone calls, paperwork, relocation costs, and miscellaneous clerical costs. Intangibles
include internal disruption, reduced efficiency and productivity, the possibility of additional turnover, and the possibility of overhiring (i.e., hiring more people than are
needed to support the workload) in an attempt to maintain
an average workforce.

An increasing shortage of qualified labor is another
problem you will have to face in your quest for qualified
workers. According to John Naisbitt and Patricia Abur-
dene, in *Re-inventing the Corporation,* by 1987 there will be
more people leaving the labor market than entering it.
Your task will also be made more difficult by the increasing
competition among companies for top-rate employees.

While there are never any guarantees that the person
you'll eventually hire will "work out," there are concrete
steps you can take to attract the best candidates, as well as
precautions that will improve your chances of making an
informed decision.

This book is designed to take you through the hiring
process step-by-step. You'll learn the techniques you'll
need for recruiting, interviewing, and selecting employees
— in fact, every aspect of effective hiring. If you follow
these guidelines, you'll be on your way to building a workforce that's qualified, talented, and motivated.

1

PREPARATION: DETERMINING WHAT YOU NEED

Before you can even think of hiring somebody for a new or existing position, you have to know what you're looking for. If you don't, you can't possibly begin to evaluate the applications you receive.

You will normally have *some* idea of the position you will be interviewing for. The better you understand the position, the better you will be able to evaluate and eliminate applications.

It should really make no difference to you whether you're filling a job that already exists or creating a new job. Even if you think you know what the position involves, it is time well spent to go through the steps outlined below to analyze your requirements. In fact, the most opportune time you will have to change the requirements of a position is when you're filling a vacancy.

The two tools that will help you do a better job of evaluating job candidates are job descriptions and job specifications. Before you begin to prepare either of these crucial instruments, however, you'll need to conduct a job analysis.

a. JOB ANALYSIS

Job analysis is a means of obtaining and recording the specific aspects of a job. A job analysis allows you to examine the responsibilities and overall makeup of a particular job so that you're better able to evaluate the types of abilities and personal characteristics necessary for that position.

1

Job analysis has been used since the 1940s. It has become more popular recently, however, as a way to avoid problems with discriminatory employment practices and to address questions of comparable worth. Because job analysis looks only at *job* characteristics, there is no built-in bias concerning the type of *individual* needed to fill a certain position. For instance, job analysis would allow you to examine the tasks involved in a secretarial or janitorial position without taking sex, height, weight, religion, nationality, or other personal characteristics into account. This is particularly important in terms of compensation for various positions (thus the link with comparable worth).

Job analysis is also important, however, when beginning the process of employee selection, and is the requisite first step in the preparation of job descriptions and job specifications. When preparing a job analysis, you first need to understand the reasons for the job's existence. From there you will need to learn more about the specific activities or duties required of the position.

1. Guidelines for job analysis

The ultimate goal of job analysis is to simplify and improve employee recruitment, training, and development. Job analysis is also an important tool in determining salary and wage rates.

To conduct a job analysis you will need to —

(a) identify the duties and responsibilities of the position,

(b) determine the qualifications required of a job holder,

(c) gather information from the current job holder and his or her superiors,

(d) observe the job holder as he or she performs the required tasks, and

(e) analyze and determine how this specific job relates to other positions within the company.

2. Sources of information

There are basically three broad means of obtaining information for a job analysis:

   (a) observing an employee as a job is performed,
   (b) interviewing the employee about the job, and
   (c) administering questionnaires asking specific questions about job duties.

In addition to these methods, or to broaden the information you receive from these methods, you might also want to ask the employee in the position to keep a log or diary of tasks performed for two to four weeks.

These methods, alone or in combination, will serve as the basis for the job analysis.

3. Suggested questions for job analysis

Whether or not you decide to use the questionnaire method, you will find the following questions helpful as you begin to analyze individual positions.

   (a) What specific tasks are performed in this position?
   (b) What machinery and/or equipment is required to perform these tasks?
   (c) What knowledge is required to fulfill the requirements of the position?
   (d) What are the expected results of the performance of this job?
   (e) What physical tasks are performed in this position?
   (f) What are the environmental conditions and demands of this position?
   (g) What are the emotional and mental demands?
   (h) How much structure is provided for this position?
   (i) How does this position relate to other positions in the company?
   (j) What special requirements does the job have (e.g., travel, overtime, etc.)?

Sample #1 shows an example of a typical job analysis.

Your completed job analysis will provide you with a summary of a job's duties and responsibilities, its relationship to other jobs, the knowledge and skills required, and any unusual working conditions. At this point you are ready to prepare the job description and job specifications.

b. JOB DESCRIPTION

A job description is a written record of a job that describes the tasks and responsibilities involved and indicates how the particular job ties in with others in the company.

In a clear, concise manner the job description should indicate job title, work performed, major job duties, minor job duties, and relationship to other jobs. Your job description should also include a section on the purpose of the job, or a job summary, and the accountabilities of the job. Specifically, your job description will include the following:

(a) Job identification (This section includes the title of the position, the date the job description was prepared, the title of the position's immediate supervisor, and (if relevant) whether the position is exempt (i.e., management) or non-exempt (i.e., non-management).)

(b) Job summary (The job summary is simply a brief description of the job which highlights the general responsibilities and characteristics of the work performed.)

(c) Job duties (This section describes the specific tasks of the position, and is described in more detail below.)

The parts or components of a job description can be divided into two broad sections: basic responsibilities and specific duties. You should first outline the specific duties and then summarize these duties into the basic responsibilities — in essence working backwards.

1. Basic responsibilities

The job description should be organized to indicate not only the responsibilities involved, but the relative importance of these responsibilities. Within the broad categories

4

Date: _____3/17/8-_____

JOB TITLE: Secretarial Clerk I

JOB DUTIES:

Major: Typing
Filing
Answering phone

Minor: Route mail
Fill in for Secretarial Clerk II when needed

RELATIONSHIPS:

Number of people supervised and relationship: N/A

Who gives work assignments: Office manager

EDUCATION/EXPERIENCE REQUIRED

High school: Diploma

College: N/A

Trade school: One year secretarial science program

Certification/License: N/A

Special schooling: N/A

On-the-job experience: Two years previous experience
in related position

KNOWLEDGE/SKILLS REQUIRED

Typing: 60 wpm
Ability to file
Pleasant phone voice

PHYSICAL REQUIREMENTS

N/A

HAZARDS/WORKING CONDITIONS

N/A

mentioned above, you will want to include information such as the following:

(a) Extent of authority exercised over the position
(b) Level of complexity of the duties performed
(c) Amount of internal and external contact
(d) Access to confidential information
(e) Amount of independent judgment required
(f) Amount of pressure on the job
(g) Type of machinery or equipment used
(h) Working conditions
(i) Terms of employment
(j) Any other significant factors peculiar to each position

2. Job duties

The job duties section is the most extensive section of the job description. It should include information on what each duty is, how it is performed, and why. The following steps will provide a clear way of organizing this section:

(a) Arrange duties in descending order of importance.
(b) Begin each statement with an action verb such as "operates," "acts," "writes," "trains," etc.
(c) Use as many objective or quantitative terms as possible and avoid generalizations.
(d) Indicate the frequency or degree of duties performed (e.g., daily, weekly, monthly, etc.).
(e) Be as specific as possible. Instead of saying "handles incoming phone calls," you should say, "answers incoming calls and directs caller to appropriate department."

Don't attempt to take down every detail of the position, but be sure to include any unusual responsibilities, even if they occur infrequently. Sample #2 shows a completed job description.

SAMPLE #2
JOB DESCRIPTION

JOB TITLE: Advertising Assistant **DATE:** 3/17/8-
DEPARTMENT OR DIVISION Advertising **STATUS:** Exempt
ACCOUNTABLE TO: Advertising Manager

JOB SUMMARY:
Assist in the development, creation, and production of advertising materials.

JOB DUTIES AND RESPONSIBILITIES
Major duties
Proofread and edit all promotional materials
Compose space advertisements
Maintain and update media information files
Monitor effectiveness of promotional activities

Minor duties
Type in-house memos, reports, and other materials as needed
Compile information and prepare reports as requested
Other job-related duties as assigned by supervisor

ORGANIZATIONAL RELATIONSHIPS:
Directly accountable to manager. Will work closely with the Graphic Design Department in the preparation of ads and other promotional materials.

After you have prepared the job description, review the information with the current job holder to be sure that it is factual, easily understood, and descriptive of the entire job. The completed job description will be used in defining the job specifications.

c. JOB SPECIFICATIONS

Job specifications are designed for the same purpose as specifications for bridges, buildings, and other structures; they indicate the materials needed to get the job done.

Job specifications describe the personal qualifications required of a job holder, including any special conditions of employment such as hazardous environmental conditions.

As you review the job description, ask yourself the following questions to help determine the specifications for the position:

(a) What is the purpose of the job?

(b) What day-to-day duties are performed?

(c) What other duties are performed?

(d) How is the position supervised?

(e) What other positions receive supervision from this position?

(f) How much, or how little, control is exercised over this position?

(g) What machines or equipment must be operated?

(h) What types of records need to be kept by this position?

(i) To what extent is this position involved in analysis and planning?

(j) What internal and external contacts are required of this position?

(k) What verbal, numerical, or mechanical aptitudes are required?

Sample #3 shows a completed job specification form.

JOB TITLE: ___Administrative Assistant___ **DATE:** ___March 17, 198-___
DEPARTMENT OR DIVISION: ___Public Relations___
ACCOUNTABLE TO: ___Vice-President, Public Relations___
STATUS: ___Exempt___

1. Diploma in secretarial/business field.
2. Minimum two years' experience in an advanced secretarial position.
3. Excellent typing ability — 80 wpm accurately.
4. Excellent machine transcription skills.
5. Pleasant telephone voice.
6. Ability to handle highly confidential business information.
7. Ability to deal effectively with time pressures, stress, and changing demands of job on a regular basis.

JOB TITLE: ___Accounting Clerk___ **DATE:** ___3/17/8-___
DEPARTMENT OR DIVISION: ___Accounting___
ACCOUNTABLE TO: ___Accounting Manager___ **STATUS:** ___Non-exempt___

1. Degree/accreditation in accounting or equivalent work experience.
2. Strong organizational ability.
3. Good data entry skill (50 wpm).
4. Ability to operate 10-key adding machine accurately.
5. Must be very detail-oriented and appreciate the value of accuracy.
6. Able to handle highly confidential business information.

d. DETERMINING THE REQUIREMENTS OF A POSITION

To determine hiring criteria, you need to examine experience, education, intelligence, and personality requirements. By establishing these requirements objectively through the use of job analysis, a job description, and job specifications, you will eliminate bias.

When formulating selection criteria you need to look at recent job performance and isolate two or three characteristics that have the most impact on successful job performance.

The requirements you set up at this point are fundamental to your recruitment efforts. Before you begin your search for qualified applicants you need to establish education, experience, physical, and mental qualifications. Answer the following questions:

(a) What level of education is necessary to perform effectively in the position? High school? College? Special training? Does this job require any type of special certificate or license?

(b) How much previous related experience should a new employee have? Will training be offered on the job?

(c) What specific physical skill is necessary? Manual dexterity? The ability to lift a certain weight?

(d) Is this a position that requires adherence to tight deadlines? Overtime? Ability to work with a variety of personality types? Ability to negotiate?

Be particularly careful that each requirement you identify is specifically job-related.

Now that you have taken these internal steps to identify and define specific requirements of the position to be filled, you are ready to move on to the next step — recruitment.

2

EFFECTIVE RECRUITMENT: HOW TO FIND THE BEST APPLICANTS

a. THE HIRING REQUEST FORM/ PERSONNEL REQUISITION

Depending on the size of your company and its internal policies, you may need to fill out a hiring request form or personnel requisition and submit it to the personnel department or to your manager or supervisor. Even if such a form is not required, it is still a helpful tool in focusing your specific hiring needs. You'll note that the sample personnel requisition (see Sample #4) asks for a job description to be attached.

b. WHERE DO YOU LOOK FOR HELP?

Whether you're adding staff in anticipation of increased human resource needs, replacing an employee who is leaving, or just thinking about the possibility of future hiring needs, your first question will be, "Where do I find the person I need?"

There are several options available to you — each offering its own advantages and disadvantages and each requiring a slightly different approach.

1. In-house

The most qualified applicant for a position, whether it has been recently vacated or newly created, may very well be a person you already have on staff.

Most companies have established procedures for internal hiring. The benefits of hiring in-house are many:

- Employee morale improves

SAMPLE #4
PERSONNEL REQUISITION

TO: Human Resources Department   DATE: _____

FROM: _____   APPROVED BY: _____

POSITION: _____   NEEDED BY: _____

_____ Addition _____ Replacement for: _____

TO BE SUPERVISED BY: _____

_____ Regular position   _____ Temporary position
                                  How long needed? _____

_____ Full time _____ Part time _____ Number of openings _____

JOB DUTIES: _____
_____
_____
_____
_____

QUALIFICATIONS NEEDED: _____
_____
_____
_____

SALARY RANGE: _____

PERSONS WHO WILL INTERVIEW APPLICANTS: _____
_____

CONDUCT SEARCH THROUGH:

_____ Internal posting   _____ Applications on file

_____ Newspaper ad   _____ Job service

_____ Newspaper ad — blind   _____ Other agencies

NOTE: Current job description is to be attached

HUMAN RESOURCE DEPARTMENT ONLY!

Filled by: _____ Date _____

Source: _____

Starting Date: _____ Rate _____

12

- Management is able to identify those employees who are interested in career advancement
- Management already knows the job history and capability of internal job candidates
- Less time is needed for employee orientation and training
- Turnover is reduced, as employees tend to look for career progression within their current company
- The company is able to make better use of its human resources

There are also disadvantages created by hiring from within:

- The number of potential job candidates is limited to qualified personnel in the company.
- The introduction of new blood is limited, sometimes resulting in insular thinking and stagnation.
- Internal recruitment always involves a "ripple effect." As one person leaves a position to fill another, a new vacancy is created. This effect continues down to the lowest level jobs which must then be filled through other means.

It is important for a company that is considering the use of an internal job posting system to establish a written procedure for implementation. The most common procedure is that when a job opening is created, all employees are notified of the position and given specific information on job title, salary, department, supervisor's name and title, responsibilities of the job, qualifications and skills required. The posting remains displayed in a prominent place for a specified number of days. The supervisor or manager doing the hiring will then review internal applicants before going outside the company. Generally, it is up to the employee to notify his or her current supervisor or manager of an application for the open position. Employees must apply for a position each time it is posted. Blanket applications are generally not accepted.

There are times when a job may not be posted, for example, when a position has been especially created for a certain employee or when a job would best be filled through a predetermined and logical career path.

The most important consideration when using a job posting system is to be fair and consistent. Morale will be reduced dramatically if employees feel that the system is administered in a biased or inconsistent manner.

2. Recruiting services

Recruiting services is a broad term covering personnel agencies, executive recruiters, headhunters, and any other agencies that perform the functions of finding, screening, and recommending candidates for a position. Besides newspaper advertising, a recruiting service is the most common means of recruiting job applicants.

The advantages of using a recruiting service are obvious. First, you save the time (and expense) of advertising, screening resumes, and conducting preliminary interviews. Second, you are able to keep the name of your company and the fact that you are hiring confidential until you actually begin the interviews. Finally, you are assured that the people you eventually do interview are qualified for the position.

Given these three important benefits, why don't more companies use recruiting services instead of doing it themselves? There are basically four reasons:

(a) Unfamiliarity with the use of recruiting services

(b) Expense (fees can range from 10% to 25% of the candidate's starting salary)

(c) Personal experience or knowledge of others' experience with disreputable agencies

(d) The belief that nobody outside the company can know the type of candidate you are looking for

These drawbacks are very real. Disreputable agencies do exist and fees can be high. If you do decide, however, to use a recruiting agency, follow these guidelines to make the experience as positive as possible.

(a) Ask around to find others who have used these services and seek recommendations. Don't hesitate to ask the agency itself for references.

(b) Ask what the cost will be. Be sure to ask about possible "hidden" fees like telephone or travel expenses.

(c) Consider working with more than one agency until you become comfortable with one.

(d) Establish a relationship and loyalty with a particular recruiter, not necessarily the agency.

(e) Be clear and specific about job requirements and candidate specifications.

(f) Be firm about your expectations of the agency and the services you expect.

3. Newspaper/trade journal ads

Running neck and neck with recruiting services, advertising is the most common recruiting method in use today and the one that is most familiar to job seekers. The elements of successful advertising for employee recruitment will be examined in more detail later in this chapter.

4. Campus recruiting

On-campus recruiting is provided as a service to students by colleges, universities, and technical schools. Many companies are taking advantage of this special opportunity to interview pre-screened, qualified individuals.

Campus recruiting is a very effective way to fill entry-level positions. To find out more about campus recruiting in your area, call the placement offices of the colleges and universities near you.

5. Recommendations and referrals

At any company there is a proliferation of recommendations and referrals from existing employees. This is certainly a way of adding applicants to your files.

Many employers view referrals as qualified leads. They take the approach that if an employee is willing to "go out on a limb" to offer the name of a friend or relative for employment, that employee is going to have a vested interest in seeing that this person performs well.

Here, as in any other means of recruitment, careful screening is essential. Never feel obligated to hire (or even interview) somebody who has been recommended to you for a position.

6. Walk-ins and unsolicited resumes

Walk-in applicants should not be dismissed out of hand. It is not at all unlikely for a qualified person to "make the rounds" in person, rather than submitting an application.

Similarly, all resumes received should be given due consideration when you're making hiring decisions. Use the same consideration for all applicants regardless of their source.

c. WHAT IS THE BEST SOURCE OF JOB CANDIDATES?

The answer to the question, "What is the best source of job candidates?" is as varied as the number of positions you have in your company.

Depending on the type of position you are trying to fill, the particular job-hunting strategies used in your geographic location, and the past experience of your company, the answer could range from college recruiting to walk-in applicants.

Keep in mind that different jobs require different recruiting methods. Following is a list of the top three means of recruiting candidates for various types of positions. Keep in mind that these are general guidelines only.

Laborers/Service Workers
1. Advertisements
2. Employee referrals
3. Walk-ins, unsolicited resumes

Clerical
1. Advertisements
2. Employment agencies
3. Employee referrals

Administrative
1. Advertisements
2. Employment agencies
3. Campus recruiting

Technical
1. Advertisements
2. Employment agencies
3. Employee referrals

Professionals
1. Advertisements
2. Employment agencies
3. Campus recruiting

Managers and executives
1. Employment agencies
2. Executive search firms

As you can see, for all positions except management and executive, advertising is the number one means of attracting qualified candidates.

Because advertising is so important to successful hiring, the next section of this chapter will look specifically at techniques for creating effective recruitment advertisements.

d. DEVELOPING EFFECTIVE RECRUITMENT ADVERTISEMENTS

The function of recruitment advertising is to attract qualified applicants. If your ads aren't on target, you're going to fail in your initial efforts at recruitment.

Before you even begin to think about how to write your ad, you need to know specifically what kind of person you're looking for. Unless you do, you won't know where to advertise, when to advertise, or how to advertise. Once you're thoroughly familiar with the job requirements and specifications as outlined in chapter 1, you're ready to begin developing your advertisements.

1. The best place to advertise

You're most likely to get a large response if you run employment ads in your weekend newspaper (Saturday or Sunday), but there are some exceptions. The *Wall Street Journal*, for instance, runs a special section on Tuesdays devoted to employment advertising. Other papers may also have special days that you should be aware of. You can bet that the job hunters are.

Most employment ads are run in the employment section of the classifieds. However, you might also consider running a display ad in another section of the paper. For instance, if you're looking for a manager or supervisor you might want to run a display ad in the business section. If you're looking for someone for real estate sales, you might advertise in the real estate section of the paper. Some papers have a separate careers listing in the business or other section of the paper for professional and managerial career opportunities.

Be innovative. And remember, there is no reason why you can't advertise in two or more sections of the same paper using a combination of approaches.

Another popular means of attracting potential employees is through the use of trade publications that are geared specifically to a certain trade or profession. The one drawback here is that most of these publications are monthly and have a long lead time for advertising space. You might have to have your ad ready three months before it will even appear in one of these publications.

Trade publications are a commonly used vehicle for employment advertising, however, and one you shouldn't overlook.

2. Open versus blind advertisements

Although blind advertisements (i.e., ads where the name of the company is not revealed) are commonly used, the consensus is that open ads draw more and better candidates for job openings. There are a few reasons for this:

(a) Blind ads rarely draw responses from people who are currently employed.

(b) Many people will not answer blind ads, so your response is dramatically decreased.

(c) Your company misses out on some public relations opportunities when you choose to use a blind ad, particularly if new positions are being created. You will help yourself in the long run by letting people know.

If blind ads are so bad, why are they used so frequently? One reason is that the company is looking outside for employees and doesn't want its current employees to know. Another reason (and, hopefully, not one you have to worry about) is that the company does not have a good reputation and potential applicants would be discouraged if its name were used.

3. What should your ad include?

There are four areas that your employment ad should cover: the type of person you're looking for, pay, benefits, and where and how to apply. You also need to be aware of equal opportunity requirements (in the U.S.) or human rights legislation (in Canada).

(a) The type of person you're looking for

If you're not clear and specific in your ad about the qualifications you expect applicants to have, you are going to be disappointed when resumes start coming in.

You need to indicate in your advertisement —

(a) the specific job skills required,

(b) experience and background required,

(c) educational requirements,

(d) travel or relocation requirements, and

(e) whether or not training will be provided.

When stating these requirements, be particularly careful to avoid the excessive use of empty adjectives like "dynamic" or "creative." Be precise and realistic. Don't exaggerate the qualifications or responsibilities of the position.

(b) Pay

Whether or not you actually state the salary for the position is up to you. However, some mention of pay should be made. You might ask applicants to submit salary expectations or simply state "competitive salary."

By stating the actual salary you will decrease the number of responses, but you won't have to worry about the possibility of losing applicants if the salary is not up to their expectations.

On the other hand, by stating the salary you may not get the opportunity to convince applicants to start at a lower rate of pay than they had expected because of the other things your company has to offer.

(c) Benefits

Company benefits can attract good candidates. Many benefits are good "draws" so be sure to include them prominently in your ad.

(d) Where and how to apply

Be specific here and be very careful that you don't omit the obvious. It is not uncommon to find an employment advertisement that says "send resume," but neglects to say where.

If you're running an open ad, you'll want to include your company's name, address, and phone number (if you're asking for call-ins). If you use a blind ad, you'll still need to indicate where resumes should be sent. Be very specific about what applicants need to do to indicate their interest in the position. Should they send in a resume? Telephone? Apply in person? Do you want to give them more than one option? Is there a time limit after which you will no longer accept applications? Spell out the details clearly to limit the chances for misunderstanding.

(e) Equal opportunity requirements (U.S.) or human rights legislation (Canada)

If you are placing an ad in the United States, you must, of course, be very careful that your advertisement does not contain any language that violates Equal Opportunity Employment Commission (EEOC) requirements. You can't make statements such as "looking for a gal Friday," or "recent college graduates please apply," or "no applicants over 40 please."

In the U.S. you should also include a simple statement of your status as an equal opportunity employer. You can simply say, "We are an equal opportunity employer (M/F)."

Similarly, in Canada such statements are prohibited by federal and provincial human rights legislation regulating discrimination in employment based on age or sex.

You might want to contact the EEOC (in the U.S.) or the federal and provincial human rights commissions (in Canada) to ensure that you are abiding by the law.

See chapter 10 for more information.

4. Tips for effective ad design

In his book *Tested Advertising Methods*, John Caples gives a formula for a successful ad: write an irresistible headline, back it up with facts, make an unbeatable offer.

This formula can just as easily be applied to employment advertising as it can to general consumer advertising. When you're advertising for employees you want to do the same thing that other major advertisers want to do: you want to encourage people to respond. There are several techniques you can use to increase the chances that they will.

(a) Use the AIDA formula

This is a classic formula for copywriters, standing for Attention, Interest, Desire, Action.

You grab the attention of the reader with striking graphics or a compelling headline. You pique interest by appealing to the reader's emotions and needs. You create desire by offering unique benefits. And you get action by asking for it.

Your headline might simply be the name of the position available. Or it could be something a bit more creative like "Special Opportunity for a Top-Notch Secretary."

Your appeal to the emotions and needs of readers will be achieved through your description of the job requirements and responsibilities. Remember that most people respond to the appeal of status, recognition, and belonging. Use these appeals in your employment ads.

Unique benefits refers to more than your health plan. What's special about this particular position? What's special about your company?

Finally, ask for action. Say, "Send in your resume now," or "Your application must be received by June 10, 198-."

(b) Find your USP

USP stands for Unique Selling Proposition. What do you have to offer that no one else has to offer — or very few others?

Do you offer special educational or training opportunities? Do you have a program for internal advancement? A unique benefit package? Are you a well-established and reputable company in the community?

You need to create an awareness of this position by differentiating it from similar positions that are available. Maybe you'll need to do some brainstorming to come up with something that sets you apart. But once you find it, be assured that you have a powerful advertising tool for recruitment of qualified applicants.

(c) Use benefits, not features

The difference between a feature and a benefit is a troubling distinction to many involved in the field of advertising. Yet this distinction is fundamental to the trade.

A benefit should tell the reader what he or she will get out of making an application for this particular position. It should answer the reader's question of "what's in it for me?"

A feature is an attribute, fact, or characteristic of your company. For instance, the fact that your company offers three weeks' paid vacation after the first year of employment is a feature. The benefit of this feature is that "you'll have plenty of free time to use after only one year with our company." Every feature yields a benefit and every benefit can be related back to a feature.

A simple test to determine whether you are offering features or benefits is to ask the question, "So?" The answer will be a benefit. For instance, "XYZ Company has been in business for over 50 years.""So?""So... when you accept a position with our company, you will share in the prestige and recognition that our product standards have brought us throughout the nation."

(d) Develop a strong headline

The headline is the most important part of your ad. It should grab readers' attention and nudge them into the copy.

Your headline should, whenever possible —

(a) include a benefit,

(b) relate to the illustration (if you're using one),

(c) feature the name of your company, and

(d) attract attention.

Chances are you'll have to write several headlines before you come up with one or two that are on target. Or you may simply decide to use the title of the position as a headline.

After you've chosen a headline, you'll find writing the body copy much easier.

(e) Think visually

Bold headlines, indented paragraphs, short copy blocks, underlining, and "bullets" are all commonly used copywriting techniques that can be incorporated into your advertisements.

Avoid designs that can hinder readability, such as reversed type (white type on black or dark background), printing on a slant, using non-serif typefaces, or printing over a picture.

If you're not familiar with design requirements, talk to a good graphic designer. It's well worth the investment. With copy *and* design working for you, you'll have an unbeatable combination.

(f) Ask for action

You can't go wrong by telling people what you want them to do. Ask for response. Tell prospective applicants what to do, why to do it, how to do it, and to do it.

An amazing number of employers fail to ask for a response. Don't be one of them. You've worked hard to get the reader's attention and lead him or her through the copy — now it's time to close the deal.

(g) Don't be afraid to try something different

"XYZ Company is doing black and white ads with almost no copy. Let's do that too."

When you're advertising, you don't want to be copying everyone else. You want to stand out from the crowd so that the positions you advertise are differentiated in the reader's mind.

If the competition is running large, four-color ads with a lot of graphics or photos, you might want to try an editorial style ad or a series of small "teaser" ads.

Whatever you do — do it your way. Don't follow the competition. Lead it.

5. Some special ideas for attracting key people

Attracting good people in today's competitive hiring market is becoming increasingly difficult and will become even more difficult in the coming years. You need to use every technique at your disposal to attract the best applicants you possibly can. Following are some tips you may find useful:

- Be especially persistent in looking for talent within your own company.
- Consider making changes in the organizational structure rather than hiring more people or replacing positions that have been vacated.
- If you do a lot of hiring, consider setting up a permanent telephone line to take inquiries about job openings.
- Ask people who currently hold the positions you're hiring for to give you recruiting ideas.
- Consider hiring people to work out of their homes.
- Use job sharing or offer special hours and flexible scheduling to attract clerical or technical people.

3

THE APPLICATION FORM
AND THE RESUME

The application and the resume go hand in hand. They are two very important tools in your recruiting efforts and you should rely on both when conducting your interviews. This is because resumes provide you with only the information the *applicant* wants you to know, while the application provides you with the information *you* need to know.

If you're running an advertisement and soliciting resumes, the resume comes first. You can then have applicants fill out application forms when they arrive for their interviews.

Walk-in candidates, who often come in without a resume, should be asked to fill out an application. Later, if these people become candidates for an open position, a resume should be requested.

a. APPLICATIONS

Your application form should be designed to provide you with the information you need to evaluate the ability, experience, skills, knowledge, and other job qualifications of people applying for employment with your company. This section discusses in detail how to design a form to match your specific needs.

Keep in mind that you may need to develop more than one form. Companies often make the error of using a blanket form for all positions. It should be obvious that the information you need before hiring a clerk is very different from the information you need before hiring a manager. Your application forms should reflect these differences.

1. What to include and why

There are a lot of questions you could ask on your application form. Some of those questions are unnecessary, however, and provide information that you really don't need until after a hiring decision has been made.

Information you should request in your application form includes the following:

(a) Applicant's name
(b) Address and phone number where applicant can be reached during the day
(c) Position applicant is applying for
(d) Prior work experience
(e) Educational experience
(f) Training or skills relevant to the position applied for
(g) Ability to work the hours required of the job
(h) Date on which the applicant will be available for work
(i) Whether the applicant is seeking full-time, part-time, temporary, or seasonal employment
(j) Whether the applicant has pertinent licenses or certification

Let's look at some of these areas in more detail.

(a) Contact information

Without information on where to contact prospective applicants, the application isn't much use. Provide space for a home phone number, a business phone number, and an address. You may also want to ask for a number where the applicant can be reached during the day or where a message can be left.

(b) Employment history

The applicant's employment history is a vital section of the application form. You want to know the name and address of every prior employer, the jobs or positions held, the job duties performed, the skills required to perform these duties, the name and title of the applicant's supervisors, the rate of pay or salary, the length and term of employment, and the reason for leaving.

This is information that you want to review carefully and thoroughly, so make sure that you allow ample space for responding to these inquiries.

(c) Special skills or knowledge

Include sufficient space on the application form to gather information about job-related skills and knowledge. Depending on the position being filled, you may want to know about typing ability, teaching experience, or supervisory skills.

(d) Job goals

You may want to include a question in the application form about the applicant's job goals. How would the applicant like to progress with the company? How does the applicant view the position being applied for in terms of his or her future career goals?

(e) Education

Again, depending on the position being filled, the information you seek will vary. Design your application form to provide you with information on schools attended, dates of attendance, overall standing or grade point average, and special achievements.

2. What not to include

For every question you come up with for your application form, ask yourself the following:

(a) Does this question need to be asked now, or could it be asked after the job is offered?

(b) Does the question refer specifically to a job-related responsibility?

If you can't answer yes, delete the question from the application form. Sample #5 shows an example of an employment application.

SAMPLE #5
EMPLOYMENT APPLICATION

Last name   First name   Initial   Telephone number

Street address   City   State/Province   Zip/Postal code

Job applied for: _____ Date: _____

Are you seeking: Full time _____ Part time _____ Temporary _____

When are you available for employment? _____ Shift preference _____

EDUCATION OR TRAINING: Please indicate your education and/or training background that is relevant to the job you are applying for:

High school

Military service, schools or training

Other training

WORK EXPERIENCE: Please list your work experience beginning with your most recent job held. If you were self-employed, give firm name.

Name of employer

Address

City, State/Province   Code

Employed from: _____ to _____

Beginning salary: Final salary: _____

Job title

Duties performed

Reason for leaving

    (Include space for additional employer information as necessary)

May we contact your present employer?   Yes _____   No _____

CERTIFICATION: My signature below certifies that all information in this application is correct and complete to the best of my knowledge and belief and that I understand that intentionally false information could result in refusal of employment or discharge. I also authorize the employers, schools or persons named above to provide information regarding my employment, education, character and qualifications.

Signature: _____ Date: _____

None of the questions on your application form should touch on an applicant's race, color, religion, national origin, age, sex, marital status, or disability. Table #1 clearly indicates what the prohibited areas of questioning are. Follow it closely as you design your application form. You cannot include any questions on these areas on your application form.

TABLE #1
PROHIBITED AREAS OF QUESTIONING

Subject	Legal	Illegal
Race		You can't ask any question referring to race or color.
Religion or creed		You can't ask any questions about religious denomination or observance of religious holidays.
National origin		You can't ask any question on lineage or nationality or any question seeking information on the applicant's parents or spouse.
Sex		You cannot ask for any indication of an applicant's sex.
Marital status		You cannot ask whether the applicant is married, divorced, or separated or for any information on the spouse or children.
Family planning		You can't ask about any plans for family — present or future.
Age	You can ask, "Are you between 18 and 70?"	You can't ask, "How old are you?"

TABLE #1 — Continued

Arrest	You can ask if an applicant has ever been *convicted* of a crime.	You can't ask if an applicant has ever been *arrested*.
Birthplace		You cannot ask for any information on applicant's birthplace or the birthplace of the applicant's parents or spouse.
Disability	You can ask about any work-related impairment.	You cannot ask, "Have you ever been treated for any of the following?"
Name	You can ask if an applicant has ever worked under another name.	You cannot ask for the maiden name of a married woman.
Photograph		You cannot ask for a photograph before employment.
Citizenship	You may ask, "Are you a citizen of this country?"	You may not ask, "Of what country are you a citizen?" or whether the applicant is a native-born citizen.
Education	You may ask about educational, vocational or professional schooling.	
Experience	You may ask about work experience.	
Military	You may ask about military service.	You may not ask about military experience in the armed forces of another country.

It is a good idea to have your application form reviewed by legal counsel before putting it to use to make sure that you complied with all legal requirements and have avoided prohibited areas of questioning.

3. Maintaining application files

Many applications get lost in the shuffle, and good applicants may never be retrieved from the personnel files. A walk-in candidate may fill out an application for a position that is not open at that time. The application is filed and two weeks or two months later, when the position opens up, the application isn't retrieved. This oversight has two potential negative outcomes:

(a) A good candidate for the job may be overlooked.

(b) The candidate may later claim that he or she has been a victim of discrimination by not being considered for a job for which he or she was qualified.

All applications that your company has on file are considered to be active unless you establish otherwise. The more applications you have on file and the more outdated they become, the greater liability you expose yourself to. There are steps you can take, however, to protect yourself:

(a) Only accept applications when you are filling a position and only for that position.

(b) When applications are being accepted, limit the time period during which they will be taken and then close off all applications.

(c) Limit the time period that you will consider an application to be active and clearly indicate to all applicants what this time period is.

(d) Keep active and inactive applications in separate files.

4. Precautions

We've already seen one way in which applications can incur potential liability for employers. There are others, and you should take the following precautions to protect yourself.

In the U.S., include the following two statements on your application form to provide yourself with some protection:

"This company is an Equal Employment Opportunity Employer and does not discriminate on the basis of color, religion, national origin, age, sex, marital status or handicap."

Directly above the signature line print, "I understand that this employment application, by itself or together with other company documents or policy statements, does not create a contract of employment. I also understand that I may voluntarily leave or be terminated at any time and for any reason."

5. Reviewing the application form

A quick review of the completed application form can alert you to potential danger signs. You should check to see if the applicant —

    (a) has had an erratic job history, with many periods of brief unemployment or job-hopping,

    (b) has left major gaps in employment unaccounted for,

    (c) has potential salary requirements that your company will be unable to meet,

    (d) has changed residence frequently,

    (e) has given past experience and educational information that is not related to the requirements of the position applied for

    (f) has given reasons for leaving previous jobs that suggest the employee may have been a problem, or

    (g) has a physical disability or health problem that would prevent him or her from performing the duties of the job.

b. RESUMES

As resumes start to look more and more alike, your task of screening those you receive becomes increasingly difficult. More and more applicants are relying on the same books, experts, and resume preparation services, so that many resumes seem to have similar formats and buzzwords.

Remember also that resumes provide you with a one-sided look at an applicant — the positive side. Resumes, by their very nature, are devised to help applicants put their best foot forward.

There is general agreement among interviewers that there is no significant correlation between the quality of a resume and the likelihood that an applicant will prove to be a good employee. You need to do more than simply read the resumes you receive; you need to be able to read between the lines to pick up on what has not been stated.

1. Key areas of the resume

There are four key areas in the resume, each providing specific information that you need to consider. These areas are career objectives, education, work experience, and personal data.

(a) Career objectives

Most applicants include a brief statement at the beginning of their resume summarizing their career or employment objectives. If the resume has been sent in response to a specific position in your company, the title of that position most often appears under career objectives, unless the applicant is sending in a pre-printed resume. In this case the stated career objective may not be as specific.

This is a good place to begin your perusal of the resume. Has somebody with a stated career objective of "administrative assistant" applied for a position as a sales manager? Is the statement very vague and open-ended, leading you to believe that the applicant doesn't have a clear goal in mind — for example, a statement such as "Interested in a challenging position with potential for personal growth"?

Be very cautious of wordy statements that include jargon and "fifty-dollar words." These statements may be intended to impress but they do not provide a good indication of a candidate's goals.

(b) Educational history

The educational history section of the resume will contain information on the level of formal education the applicant has attained and may also include specific courses taken, specialized training programs or professional development workshops, and standing or grade point average.

It is interesting to note that the length and detail of the educational history section of the resume varies in inverse proportion to the length and detail of the experience section. When the educational section is long and detailed, the experience section is generally short or nonexistent. Where the experience section is long and detailed, the education section is generally brief.

Recent college graduates are usually the applicants lacking depth in experience. They tend to expand on the educational section and often provide information that is very detailed but of little use to the interviewer. People who have been in the workforce longer, on the other hand, put more emphasis on their work accomplishments.

When reviewing the educational history section of the resume, look for an educational background that clearly meets the requirements of the position. Look for supplemental education, too, especially where it indicates a clear progression and interest in the area of training that corresponds to the job opening.

(c) Work experience

This section of the resume is the one you should be most interested in. Here is where you find specifics on the applicant's qualifications, experience, and career progression.

The most important things to be on guard for are unexplained gaps in employment or frequent job changes that do not indicate progression.

This is an area that lends itself to filler material. You have to be particularly careful not to fall prey to colorful language and cleverly devised descriptions of job responsibilities that are vague and meaningless.

(d) Personal data

The personal section of the resume can often be a surprising treasure-trove of information. Participation in civic groups or volunteer activities indicates ambition and "other-centeredness." Specific hobbies related or similar to job responsibilities can indicate a particularly strong interest in the line of work being applied for.

A note of caution to American readers: it is a good idea to have somebody in your organization in charge of screening all applications that come into the company and cutting or blacking out information that is prohibited by EEOC guidelines. Such things as date of birth, marital status, height and weight should be deleted from the resume. Photos submitted with resumes should be removed.

References are also a common inclusion in resumes. References are discussed in chapter 7.

2. What to look for

When reviewing the resumes you receive, you should be looking for more than facts. You should be looking for specific signs or indications of potential achievement, such as the following:

(a) Profit-mindedness (Does the applicant highlight areas in which duties or responsibilities in previous positions contributed to or affected the bottom line?)

(b) Stability and career direction (Frequent job changes don't necessarily portend disaster. If a progression is evident through these job changes it may simply indicate that the applicant is aggressive and career-minded. Conversely, a long stint in one job is not necessarily good. If no progression is evident, this apparent stability may be an indicator of low motivation.)

(c) Use of specific descriptions (Beware of generalities. The more general an applicant's description is, the more likely he or she is inflating job responsibilities and achievements. Look for specific, quantifiable examples of demonstrated success — both educational and work-related.)

(d) Ambition (Look for evidence that the candidate is a hard worker, willing to do more than is required of the average employee. Do the job responsibilities the candidate has listed in a previous position as a file clerk, for example, seem to extend beyond the scope of what is normally required of that type of position? This may be a sign of the candidate's ability to work

hard and willingness to accept increased
responsibility.)

3. Danger signals

As you are wading through the resumes you've received
you'll also want to be aware of danger signals. First, be on
guard for slick resumes. Don't be taken in by gloss. Look
beyond the surface appearance of the resume to the information presented. Beware of lengthy descriptions of education that may hide a lack of experience. All you really
need is an indication of skills attained and degrees earned.

Also, watch for gaps in background. Some resumes are
prepared in functional rather than chronological form.
This format makes it easy to hide or completely leave out
gaps in education or experience.

Overuse of general terms such as "knowledge of,"
"experience with," or "exposure to" is another danger sig-
nal. You need to look for indications of hands-on
experience.

Finally, if you sense any anger as you read the resume,
beware. Chances are that if anger shows through in a
resume it will certainly surface on the job.

4. Narrowing it down

Now that you find yourself faced with a formidable pile of
applications and resumes, it's time to sift through the
responses and identify those that show the most promise
— the applicants you will eventually want to interview.

You should have a system in place as you review the
resumes you've received. A common system used by many
interviewers is to sort the resumes into three piles: definites, maybes, and nos. You can set up interviews with the
definites and write letters of rejection to the nos. You
should also interview some of the maybes just to give
yourself a feel for your own objectivity and the validity of
your selection criteria.

Before you begin, however, you will need to go back and
review the hiring criteria you established in chapter 1. As
you compare the qualifications of candidates to the criteria

you have selected, you may find it helpful to use a selection grid. By making the process as objective as possible you can avoid some of the bias that often creeps into selection decisions.

Sample #6 is an example of a selection grid. You can insert candidates' names down the left side of the chart; selection criteria can be indicated along the top. You can score each criterion on a scale of 1 to 10, 10 being the optimal score. Alternatively, you may want to write down a few words in each category, commenting on the candidate's suitability in each.

5. Using the resume to structure the interview

As you review each resume, have the job specifications and requirements in mind (see chapter 1). Jot down questions that arise and areas where you will need to ask applicants for clarification. Here are some questions that might arise:

(a) Why are there gaps in your educational (or employment) history? What did you do during these periods that aren't accounted for on the resume?

(b) Why is there a shift in your educational emphasis?

(c) Why is there a shift in your career emphasis?

(d) Why have you changed jobs so frequently?

(e) Why are you making a career change at this time?

(f) Why are your career ambitions so different from your educational achievements?

(g) As you consider your career progression to date, where do you see yourself heading?

6. Guarding against resume falsification

Unfortunately, some people lie on their resumes. As an employer, you need to be aware of this and know how you can protect yourself from being deceived.

One applicant may have attended three years of college but never graduated. He writes in his resume that he received a B.A. Another candidate received a B.A. and always intended to go on for a Master's. She writes that she received an M.A. Yet another candidate never received any formal education and considers it a sore spot — a blight in the midst of his otherwise excellent qualifications. He feels

SAMPLE #6
SELECTION GRID

Applicant	Education	Experience	Verbal Ability	Salary Requirement	(Other)	(Other)	(Other)
Sara Smith	2	10	5	8			
Jim Jones	10	2	5	5			
Fred Flint	8	8	7	8			
Ruth Riddle	7	5	3	10			
Joan Johnson	6	6	6	6			
•							
•							
•							
•							
•							
•							
•							
•							
•							
•							
•							
•							
•							
•							
•							
•							
•							
•							

*Score on a scale of 1–10 — 10 being optimal score.

his experience has given him the equivalent (or better) of a formal education. His resume indicates not only that he received a B.A., but that he graduated in the top 10% of his class.

The best way to protect yourself is to check the information given to you. Top universities get several calls a week from employers attempting to verify that applicants have attended there.

Applicants who lie are banking on the hope that you, like many other prospective employers, won't check their claims. Chapter 7 discusses ways you can check into educational and work backgrounds as well as personal and professional references.

7. How to use the application and resume during the interview

You can, and should, make extensive use of both the application and the resume *before* the actual interview. But once the interview begins, you should put them aside.

The application and resume are the basis of the interview, but the interview itself should be structured to delve into the gray areas that haven't been fully addressed by either of these forms. Most job applicants find it insulting to be asked to reiterate points they have already covered in their resume or on the application form. Moreover, using these props during the interview prevents you from developing a conversational interview approach.

4

THE INTERVIEW: AN OVERVIEW

a. THE PURPOSE OF AN INTERVIEW

A job interview is actually little more than an opportunity for an employer and a prospective employee to get to know each other. There are three primary purposes to a job interview:

(a) For the interviewee to demonstrate job-related skills and qualifications

(b) For the interviewer to tell the applicant about the job and the company

(c) For the interviewer to gather more information about the applicant than the resume provided

As an interviewer, you're going to want to determine if the applicant is qualified for the job, how well the applicant will fit in with the company, to what extent the applicant will be able to grow in the company, and if it would be a benefit to the company to hire the applicant.

A job interview is intended to narrow the number of likely prospects for a job. Keep this thought foremost in your mind as you begin the quest for employees.

b. TYPES OF INTERVIEWS

The type of interview you conduct will depend both on the job you're interviewing for and on the interviewing procedures your company has established.

There are five types of interviews: the patterned interview, the conversational interview, the comprehensive interview, the stress interview, and the group interview.

1. The patterned interview

The patterned interview is a structured situation where questions are standard and predetermined. This type of interview allows the interviewer to cover specific areas and identify personal strengths and weaknesses of the candidate. Specific, systematic answers regarding an applicant's qualifications and experience can be obtained in a patterned interview.

(a) Advantages

For the interviewer the patterned interview is relatively easy to prepare and conduct. Since questions are standard and the information looked for is generally specific and quantitative, screening may also be less difficult.

(b) Disadvantages

For today's more sophisticated applicant, the patterned interview is often too structured, too impersonal. This type of interview does not, therefore, work well when hiring for middle- or upper-level positions.

2. The conversational interview

The conversational interview is often what many interviewers end up conducting — after they fail to prepare. It is an unplanned, haphazard discussion that progresses with no clear direction and leaves the interviewer still needing additional information to make a hiring choice.

Why would you want to use this type of interview? You wouldn't, unless you're hiring sales representatives or filling other people-oriented positions where you want to assess the applicant's conversational style. The conversational interview might then serve as a prelude to a more structured interview.

3. The comprehensive interview

The comprehensive interview is the most widely used and successful interviewing technique. It is a combination of the informal conversational interview and the patterned interview.

In the comprehensive interview, the interviewer has a definite plan to follow, but also allows for deviations from the plan so important details can be explored further.

Discussion is encouraged through this participative approach and respect is shown for each applicant. With today's more sophisticated applicant, this is often the best approach to take.

4. The stress interview

The stress interview is becoming an increasingly popular choice for executive interviews. The purpose of the stress interview is to put the applicant under pressure to determine how well he or she will cope.

The technique used is to catch the applicant off guard and gauge the response. Questions are asked on subjects far afield from the topic of discussion. For instance, while questioning an applicant about achievements at a past job, the interviewer might ask, "What's your favorite television program?"

Unfortunately, there is little evidence to suggest that stress interviews are effective for measuring stress tolerance. Ratings are very subjective, especially when the interview is being conducted by a relatively inexperienced interviewer.

In addition, the use of this type of tactic may make it more difficult to explore other facets of the candidate's abilities, as the candidates in stress interviews often become more defensive and guarded. Since one of the goals in an interview is to put the candidate at ease, the stress interview should rarely be your choice.

Stress-type questions are also often asked during conversational or comprehensive interviews.

5. Group interviews

If more than one person will be making the final selection decision, a group interview is the logical choice. The interviewers may be representatives of the personnel department, management, or even peers.

An advantage of a group interview is that you will have a number of perspectives on which to base your final decision.

There are, however, two important disadvantages:

(a) A group situation will automatically place the candidate under a certain amount of stress.

(b) When peers are involved, there may be a tendency for them to view applicants as competition.

Depending on the position you're hiring for, the philosophy of your company, and your own particular style, you may decide to use any of the above five types of interviews. Keep in mind, however, the disadvantages that are associated with some of them, particularly the conversational and stress approaches.

c. STAGES OF THE INTERVIEW

Each interview proceeds in stages, much like the scenes in a play. Each stage has its own purpose and is intended to accomplish certain goals. An awareness of the purpose of each stage and the goals you are to accomplish makes the entire process much more smooth and trouble-free.

There are three stages that each interview goes through: the opening, the data exchange, and the closing.

1. Opening

There are four objectives you need to accomplish during the opening phase of the interview. How well you accomplish these objectives determines how well the remainder of the interview proceeds.

During the opening of the interview you want to put the applicant at ease, establish the objective of the interview, explain how the interview will proceed, and exchange enough information to allow you both to determine if the interview should continue.

(a) Putting the applicant at ease

Before you begin the interview, you want to make the applicant feel welcome and comfortable. As in any social situation, you want to exercise the usual amenities: shake hands, take the applicant's coat, offer the applicant a chair and coffee if appropriate, introduce yourself, and begin with some informal discussion.

(b) Explaining the objective of the interview

You need to set the stage for what is to follow to provide both you and the applicant with a frame of reference for the interview.

You may say something like, "The objective of this interview is to determine how your interests and qualifications fit in with our company's needs."

(c) Outlining how the interview will proceed

Again, your purpose is to make the applicant comfortable by making this meeting seem a bit more familiar and a little less unknown and frightening. Tell the applicant what you intend to do during the meeting, approximately how long you think it will take, and what your expectations of the applicant are.

You might say, "I'll be asking you some questions about your background and experience, telling you a bit about the company and the position, and offering you the opportunity to ask any questions that you might have."

If you plan to give any tests or ask the candidate to demonstrate any job-related skills, this is the time to mention it.

(d) Determining a shared frame of reference

If, for some reason, the candidate is not interested in this particular position or didn't understand exactly what was going to ensue, you want to know that now before you both waste time going through the rest of the interview.

You might say something like, "To make sure we're both clear on what we intend to accomplish today, why don't you tell me what you know about ABC Company and what you understand this position to be." In this way you'll get a better idea of the applicant's expectations and make sure that the applicant understands the way in which the interview will proceed.

2. Data exchange

The data exchange is the meat of the interview. This is the stage where you gather the information you need to make a selection. Obviously, the way you conduct the data exchange is crucial. You need to ask the appropriate questions, solicit pertinent responses, and constantly evaluate the applicant's verbal and non-verbal expression.

During the data exchange you gather information on work history, educational background, and professional goals.

(a) Work history

In the area of work history there are several things you will want to explore —

- Specific duties and responsibilities in prior positions
- Accomplishments at previous jobs
- Progress in terms of promotions, pay increases, or added responsibilities
- Failures and how they were handled
- What the applicant liked and disliked about each of the previous jobs held
- The reasons for leaving each previous position

(b) Educational background

When exploring educational background you want to know —

- What education beyond high school the applicant has
- When and where post-secondary degrees or diplomas (if any) were obtained
- How successful the applicant was
- What the applicant's best and worst subjects were
- What extracurricular activities the applicant was involved in
- How the applicant's education was financed
- If education was an enjoyable experience or if it was something the applicant felt forced into

(c) Professional goals

An important aspect of any interview is determining what the applicant's personal and professional goals are. You want to know —

- What the applicant considers to be his or her outstanding achievements
- What the applicant's long-range career goals are

3. Closing
After you have solicited all the information you need to make a hiring choice, it is time to close the interview. At this time you want to tie up any loose ends, allow for questions from the applicant, and establish a system for follow-up.

(a) Tying up loose ends
The interview is a stress-filled process for both the applicant and the interviewer. It is quite possible that you may have neglected to obtain some important information. Now is the time to get that information. Review your notes and take a few moments to recap the interview with the applicant to make sure you have covered all the pertinent information and gathered the responses you need to make a decision.

(b) Applicant questions
After the applicant has answered all of your questions, and you have had the opportunity to explain what the position involves and provides information about the company, you should solicit questions. Some things that the applicant feels are relevant may not have been covered. The applicant may often be able to provide you with important additional information that you failed to solicit.

(c) Establishing a system for follow-up
Let the applicant know when you expect to make a decision and how he or she will be contacted. Will you be conducting second interviews? Contacting the applicant's references? Be clear about the steps you intend to take to set the applicant at ease about the waiting period that will follow the interview. Be careful, however, not to say anything that could be construed as a job offer.

d. THE EXPERIENCED APPLICANT

Many of the applicants you will interview are very familiar with the interview process — perhaps even more familiar than you are. Consider that many applicants have not only participated in other interviews, but have probably read information in magazines and books about how to prepare for interviews and how to field tough questions. In addition, many educational institutions offer placement services designed to help students be good interviewees.

You need to be on guard for the sophisticated applicant who has heard all of the questions and knows the answers you want to hear. This means you must be able to see beyond the gloss of glib answers and a polished presentation to the meat of the responses — the specifics on which you will base your decision.

5

THE INTERVIEW TECHNIQUE

a. DEVELOPING AN INTERVIEW APPROACH

The approach you take in an interview is determined in large part by your personality. The four types of approaches dealt with here are directive, nondirective, inductive, and deductive.

1. The directive approach

With the directive approach to questioning you determine in advance what questions you will ask and how you will phrase the questions to elicit the information you need. The directive approach is very structured and is a good way to obtain factual information. The responses you get with this approach will usually be straightforward yes or no responses.

2. The nondirective approach

In nondirective interviews, the applicant takes the lead and the interviewer encourages discussion, much like a counseling situation. Open-ended questions are used here rather than questions requiring a yes or no response.

A nondirective approach is felt to be more effective in revealing the applicant's feelings, therefore providing a broader base of information from which to make a selection decision. However, you need to be especially careful to maintain control, as a nondirective approach can sometimes cause the interview to lose focus.

3. The inductive approach

Inductive questioning proceeds from the specific to the general. With this type of questioning you would typically begin with a directive series of questions calling for specific, objective information and proceed to more nondirective questions requiring open-ended responses from the applicant.

4. The deductive approach

Deductive questioning proceeds from the general to the specific. You begin the interview questions in a general vein, using nondirective questioning to elicit somewhat subjective responses. From here you proceed to more specific, directive questions to gather factual information.

b. DEVELOPING RAPPORT

Your biggest challenge during the interview is to develop rapport with the applicants you meet. When you develop good rapport with the applicants, you establish a climate that allows them to reveal negative as well as positive information.

The first important consideration in establishing rapport is the setting for the interview. Make sure that you have chosen a place that is quiet, comfortable, and private. You should not be vulnerable to any interruptions during the interview, either from walk-in visitors or phone calls.

When applicants arrive, be prompt. Don't leave them cooling their heels in the reception area unless you are trying to gauge their behavior under pressure. In that case you may have asked the receptionist to let you know how the applicant responded to a wait of 5 or 10 minutes.

As you greet the applicant, be friendly and make eye contact. Introduce yourself, show the applicant to your office, offer him or her a seat, and make sure the person is comfortable. If the candidate is not relaxed and at ease, you will not get an accurate portrait of his or her normal behavior.

Before you begin the interview, spend a few minutes in small talk to break the ice. Any topic will do as long as it involves a casual, neutral subject. Keep in mind that you will be most successful in building rapport if you can get the applicant to do most of the talking.

As you conduct the interview you should take notes. Note-taking does not need to be a stressful experience for the applicant. Keep the note pad on your lap as you jot down key responses to your questions and impressions of the applicant. Be as unobtrusive as possible. If the applicant is discussing a sensitive matter, stop taking notes until after the topic changes. You can catch up later.

As the interviewer, it is your job to guide the interview and keep the applicant at ease. If you sense that the applicant's anxiety level is rising, you may want to change the course of your questioning. As you head into more sensitive areas you can gauge how well the applicant is responding and proceed accordingly.

Many of the techniques that are traditionally used in psychological counseling situations can also be applied effectively to the interview situation. These techniques can be either behavioral or verbal.

1. Behavioral encouragement

Attentiveness is an important aspect of your behavior that the applicant will quickly pick up on. When you ask a question, do you listen carefully for the response and give the impression that you are sincerely interested in what is being said, or do you act in an impatient and preoccupied manner? Your animation and enthusiasm is important in soliciting responses from the applicants you interview.

Other behavioral cues that will encourage applicants to keep talking are smiles, nods, leaning forward slightly in your chair, and maintaining direct eye contact. Even silence can be an important behavioral cue. Make sure that you are giving applicants adequate time to answer your questions — don't jump in too quickly if there is a silent moment.

2. Verbal encouragement

Praise, encouragement, and supportive comments will help you maintain a continuing flow of information from the applicant. Statements such as "I see," "I understand," "good," or "yes" are all good encouragers. Non-words like "mmmm," "ahhh," or "unh huh" are also good.

In addition, you may want to use clarifying statements. When an applicant responds to a question, you may want to repeat the response and preface it with, "You're saying that . . . " or, "As I understand it . . . ." Neutral phrases such as "Tell me more about it" or "Go on" are also good ways to keep the conversation going.

Remember that the applicant should be doing most of the talking. You are merely the facilitator. It's your job to elicit as complete a response as possible.

c. EFFECTIVE LISTENING TECHNIQUES

Ask any businessperson what the number one problem is in management and you'll get the same answer — communication. Poor communication is at the root of every business problem, from low productivity to employee theft. And at the root of most communication problems is poor listening.

When you're interviewing for a position, you can't afford not to listen — and listen effectively. That means paying more than "ear service" to the applicants you're interviewing. To improve your listening skills, you need to be aware of some of the problems that can prevent good listening.

1. Hearing only what you expect to hear

After you've conducted a number of interviews you may become very familiar with the responses you receive to certain questions. So familiar, in fact, that you tend to tune out after you ask one of these questions. You may fall into the habit of automatically nodding with a knowing smile because you know, or think you know, what's going to be said next. Or you may consciously or unconsciously ignore information that you didn't expect to hear.

2. Becoming confused by conflicting information

Sometimes what you hear isn't consistent with your preconceptions of the speaker. You may have already formed an opinion about the applicant from the resume or from other information you have. When you hear a message that conflicts with your previous beliefs, your beliefs will usually override the message. Consequently, you come away with a validation of what are often inaccurate perceptions.

3. Letting biases interfere

We all have biases to some degree. If we like somebody (usually if they're very much like us), we're more likely to listen to what they have to say than if we dislike this person. In fact, even negative information is more readily accepted from those we like and respect.

Biases also affect the way we view the information we're being given. If education is very important to you, what will your perception be of a job candidate who barely managed to graduate from high school and readily admits that "school just isn't my thing"?

4. Emotions

Mood is a major determinant of how well we listen. If we're relaxed, we'll absorb more. If we've had a rough day, or have a million other things on our minds, we won't pay close attention to what's being said to us.

5. Tips for effective listening

Following are some easy-to-use, yet effective, tips:

- Make a positive, sincere effort to listen.
- Use feedback. Make sure that what you think you heard is actually the message the sender intended you to receive.
- Comment on nonverbal cues you're picking up, especially if you're getting mixed messages.
- Physically remove yourself from noise that might impede the communication process. Make sure that you will be free from any disruptions or distractions.
- Be a committed listener. Don't allow your mind to wander.
- Be open-minded. Don't let personal biases interfere with the message you're being sent.

- Make notes. This is especially important as one applicant's qualifications fade into another's.
- Notice your own reactions without being absorbed in them. Be other-directed. Pay close attention to the people you interview — both verbally and nonverbally.

d. OBSERVING NONVERBAL CUES

In the interviews you conduct it will often be not so much what is said as what is left unsaid that determines your reactions and perceptions. The nonverbal cues you receive are an important means of evaluating the verbal information you're hearing.

1. Facial expression

The face is the most expressive part of the body. It has been estimated that we can make and recognize nearly 250,000 distinct facial expressions. The most common of these are interest, enjoyment, surprise, distress, shame, contempt, anger, and fear.

Eye contact is, perhaps, the single most important mode of nonverbal communication. In a conversation, eye contact may vary from 25% to 100%. When we are talking, eye contact is reduced, while it is increased substantially when we are listening. Too much eye contact may become dominating, while too little may show a lack of strength or purpose. For instance, we may say that somebody "looked us squarely in the eye," meaning they were assertive.

In addition to eye contact, a furrowed brow, quivering chin, twitching or flared nostrils, or a telltale blush all lend themselves to easy recognition and interpretation.

2. Body language

Our bodies also have the potential to convey various messages. Language experts agree that there are five basic body areas: center, head, posture, hands, and legs.

The total image is important. Before making judgments, you must focus on the sum of the parts. For instance, a smiling face means nothing if it is accompanied by a cold stare and clenched fists. Conversely, we may shake our fists in jest at somebody with a genuine smile on our face.

3. Interpreting nonverbal cues

To become more effective at reading and interpreting the nonverbal cues around you, consider the following suggestions:

(a) It is often difficult to "read" somebody we don't know very well. A baseline of a person's average expressions and reactions is needed before interpreting gestures with any accuracy. Keep this in mind as you attempt to interpret the nonverbal reactions of applicants who, in most cases, you do not know well.

(b) Keep in mind that you do not know the context of the interview for the applicant. What happened to the applicant immediately prior to the interview? What would your reaction be? Because some facial expressions are so close — consider the expressions for fear and surprise, for example — you may make incorrect assumptions unless you are aware of the context.

(c) Since emotions are fleeting you must be able to pick up very rapid expressions. Keep in mind that many facial expressions are blends of two or more feelings.

(d) When possible, check your interpretations of nonverbal cues. This can avoid misunderstandings resulting from incorrect conclusions.

e. TIPS TO MAKE YOUR INTERVIEW FOOLPROOF

In the last two chapters we've covered the parts of an interview and specific guidelines for developing rapport and listening effectively to both verbal and nonverbal information. Here are some additional tips that can aid you in conducting the employment interview:

(a) Have a plan for the interview before you begin. Determine in advance what type of interview you will be conducting and what questioning approach you will take.

(b) Follow a logical sequence in your questioning. Don't jump back and forth from one major area to another.

(c) Create a comfortable interview environment.

(d) Put the applicant at ease immediately and keep up the rapport throughout the interview.

(e) Keep your reactions to yourself. Learn to guard your own nonverbal responses.

(f) Take notes. You won't be able to effectively remember all the details about each applicant without them.

(g) Don't oversell the position. Present the position and the company accurately.

(h) Learn something from each experience and pinpoint ways you can improve your interviewing style.

6

DEVELOPING YOUR
QUESTIONING SKILLS

a. QUESTIONING SKILLS

Since the body of the interview involves data exchange, your effectiveness at questioning skills is extremely important. This is the most difficult part of conducting an interview and a part that many interviewers fail miserably. You can, however, learn effective questioning techniques to draw out the information you need.

Questioning may seem like a simple skill. It is not. Your skill in questioning the applicants you interview will determine whether or not you gather all the pertinent information you need.

Interviewers who are able to keep an applicant talking have mastered a fine art. They are the interviewers who manage to dig out the hidden bits of information that can make or break the interview. They are also the interviewers who seem time and again to choose employees who are both effective and efficient in the positions for which they are hired.

To be effective at questioning, even before you become familiar with the specific types of questions (see section b.), you need to be aware of some critical factors.

1. Know what you want to know

It's pure folly to go into an interview with no idea of the direction you want to take. If you haven't mapped out a specific questioning strategy and determined the information you'll need, you can't possibly expect to ask the right questions.

The kind of information you'll want to gather will depend on the position you're interviewing for. You should be very familiar with the qualifications the position requires of a job holder. You'll also need to know how to solicit the responses that will allow you to determine whether specific candidates have these qualifications.

2. Outline a plan of action

If you haphazardly jump from one area of questioning to another, you'll not only confuse and irritate the applicants you're interviewing, you're likely to confuse yourself as well.

Follow a natural progression of data gathering. The most typical progression proceeds from work history to educational background to personal and professional goals. You may decide for various reasons to follow a different progression. The important thing is that the interview proceeds smoothly from one area to another.

3. Don't ask unnecessary questions

It's not at all uncommon for interviewers to blithely embark on a line of questioning that covers virtually verbatim the information that has already been supplied in the resume or on the application form.

If all you're going to do is rehash information you already have, you could have saved yourself and the job applicants a lot of time by making a decision based solely on that information. You'll want to use the resume as a guide, of course. But you'll be trying to fill in between the lines, not to get the applicant to repeat information you've already been provided with.

4. Maintain control

While you don't want to rush applicants in and out of your office in assembly line fashion, you also don't want to let them ramble on for hours.

You don't have to be rude or abrupt to keep the interview on track. You're in the position of control, and your applicants will expect you to indicate when they have answered a question to your satisfaction. Don't be too timid to intervene when an applicant strays off on a tangent. You can say something like, "Let's get back to . . . " or "You've answered my question about _____ , now let's go on to . . . ."

b. FIVE TYPES OF QUESTIONS

There are five broad categories of questions that you may use during an interview. Each type has specific advantages and disadvantages.

1. Closed-ended questions

Closed-ended questions are those questions that elicit yes/no answers or factual responses. An example of a closed-ended question would be "Do you like clerical work?" The job applicant can only respond with a simple yes or no. The interviewer, consequently, doesn't gain much from the exchange.

An example of a question eliciting a factual response would be "How long did you work for ABC Company?" Since the applicant can only answer with a quick factual answer, the interviewer doesn't gain a great deal of information.

Questions that start with the words do, have, is, was, would, did, had, are, were, and could produce a closed-ended response.

The disadvantages of closed-end questions are obvious. They provide very little information and often force polar responses — since the applicant either agrees or disagrees, everything is black and white, and you don't get any shades of gray or variations of response.

Closed-ended questions aren't all bad, however. They allow you to get specific answers, they are easy to tabulate, and they require less effort for the respondent.

It's quite possible that after asking an applicant a series of questions that require a great deal of thought and lengthy response, you might want to throw in a few closed-ended questions to provide a respite. In general, however, if you want to keep the conversation flowing during the interview, avoid closed-ended questions.

2. Open-ended questions

An open-ended or broad question is one that expands the range of applicant responses and requires a thoughtful answer. They are good for exploring attitudes, philosophies, and areas in which it is difficult to be specific. Open-ended questions allow you to determine how the applicant thinks, how well the applicant communicates, and how well the applicant is able to organize and structure responses.

By allowing the applicant to structure responses in his or her own way, you create a nondefensive atmosphere. You also place the burden of responsibility for carrying the conversation on the applicant by asking questions that encourage free verbalization.

Questions that begin with the words who, what, where, when, why, and how solicit open responses. Open-ended questions might also start with a phrase such as "Tell me . . . ."

Closed-ended questions can easily be converted to open-ended questions. Here are some examples:

Closed: How long did you work for ABC Company?
Open: Tell me about your employment with ABC Company.

Closed: Have you had any sales experience?
Open: What type of sales experience have you had?

Closed: Do you mind working overtime?
Open: How do you feel about working overtime?

Closed: Are you good at handling stress?
Open: When you're under a lot of stress, what do you do?

When using open-ended questions, you may be asked by an applicant, "What exactly do you want to know?" Your response should be "I don't have anything special in mind. Whatever you'd like to tell me would be fine," or "Just tell me anything that you think would be helpful."

Don't be put off by silence. Four seconds of silence can seem like an eternity. But resist the impulse to fill the void. Be patient.

The value of the open-ended question can be ruined if you interrupt the applicant's train of thought. The only exception to the "no-interruption" rule is if the applicant goes off on a tangent. Then you'll want to gently guide the conversation back to the specific area you're exploring.

One disadvantage of open-ended questions is that you may not get the answer you need. This simply requires persistence on your part and you may need to rephrase the question or probe for more detail.

Some examples of probing questions are "Could you explain what you meant by . . . ?", "Could you please tell me more about . . . ?", and "How did you feel about that?"

3. Leading questions

Many interviewers inadvertently give away the answers they're looking for by feeding the answers to the applicant through the phrasing of the questions they ask, as in these examples:

"I'm sure you wouldn't mind working Saturdays, would you?"

"What exactly do you like about working with numbers?" (when the applicant hasn't even indicated that he or she likes working with numbers)

Avoid leading questions at all costs. Review your questions in advance to make sure that they do not indicate to your applicants the response you're looking for. You're not trying to spoonfeed answers, you're trying to solicit accurate information.

4. Sensitive questions

In every interview you will be asking some questions that an applicant might consider sensitive. Specific approaches to sensitive areas are addressed later in this chapter. For now, we'll look broadly at the technique for asking sensitive questions. You will certainly want to explore some delicate and potentially threatening areas with certain applicants.

Your being able to ask sensitive questions effectively presupposes that you have established a climate of rapport during the interview. Once you have developed an atmosphere of trust and mutual respect, you're ready to move into more delicate areas of questioning.

Suppose one of the people you're interviewing has been fired from the last job. You will want to know why. But you won't want to tactlessly blurt out, "Why were you fired?" You'll want to lead into the question carefully in a non-threatening manner.

You might handle this sensitive area by beginning with a qualifying statement:

"It isn't uncommon for employees to have a few things that they dislike about their manager. What were some of the things you found troubling about your last employer?"

or

"I understand that you were released from your last job. I know there are any number of reasons that an employer decides to lay off an employee. Could you tell me what the circumstances were in your case?"

The important factor when asking sensitive questions is to maintain a climate of support and acceptance. What you reveal nonverbally is as important as what you say verbally. Guard your reactions carefully so that you aren't projecting an attitude of disapproval or censure.

5. Hypothetical questions

Hypothetical questions may very well be the best questions you can ask to get at the specific qualifications of the job you're hiring for. They are also the questions that require the most creativity and forethought to develop effectively.

When asking hypothetical questions you are not necessarily looking for a specific answer, but are trying to understand the process used by the applicant to arrive at an answer. Here's an example:

"A supervisor has been lenient in letting staff members come in after 8:00 a.m., satisfied that the work will be done and that the employees will stay late if necessary. Now this supervisor's manager is applying pressure to get these people to work on time. How would you evaluate this situation? What would you do if you were the supervisor?"

Hypothetical questions provide a wide range of responses that are behavior-oriented. They are one of the best ways of exploring an applicant's judgment and decision-making skills and have been shown to have high predictive value.

Two cautions:

(a) Be careful not to lead the applicant with your question.

(b) Be sure the question you ask addresses a specific aspect of the job that you feel will be a good indicator of job performance.

c. HANDLING SENSITIVE AREAS EFFECTIVELY

We've already taken a broad look at the area of sensitive questioning. Now we'll look more specifically at how you can incorporate pointed questions into your interviews. When you're trying to delve into sensitive personal data you need to be extremely careful that you don't damage the rapport you've built, thereby losing the opportunity to obtain this information.

The best time to begin examining sensitive areas is about three-quarters of the way through the interview, after good rapport has already been established and the applicant feels at ease.

Here are some tips for handling sensitive areas:

- Keep questions open-ended.
- Speak the applicant's language. Don't be unnecessarily lofty or obviously condescending.
- Don't allow yourself to respond negatively to responses made by the applicant. Maintain a non-judgmental posture throughout the interview.
- After asking a particularly threatening question, follow the question with a few nonthreatening questions before going on to another threatening one.

- You can soften direct questions by beginning with qualifying statements such as "Is it possible . . . ?", "How did it happen that . . . ?", and "Why, in your opinion, . . . ?"

It's important that you let applicants know that they can talk safely about sensitive areas without causing you to form negative impressions that will jeopardize their hiring potential.

Be specific and ask only about those areas that directly relate to the position you're interviewing for.

d. COMMON ERRORS WHEN DEVELOPING QUESTIONS

Your development of effective questions for the selection interview is a crucial aspect of effective hiring. Yet many interviewers are hampered because they fall into the following very common traps.

1. Choosing a set of generic questions and using them for all job openings

While there are some standard questions that you can build your interview around, you should not fall into the trap of asking all candidates (regardless of the position applied for) the same questions.

A candidate for a secretarial position will naturally need to be asked different questions than a candidate for a managerial position. You'd be surprised, however, at the number of interviewers who simply pull out their standard list of questions whenever they have to conduct an interview.

2. Asking all candidates for the same position the same questions

While you want to develop a set of questions you will use for your interviews, you will occasionally want to stray beyond the list so you can explore specific aspects of a particular candidate's background.

3. Asking questions that are not related to job duties

It is commonly agreed that one of the best ways to avoid the possibility of legal problems when interviewing is to never ask any question that is not directly related to the performance of the job.

Thus, if you're interviewing for a Sunday delivery person, you can ask your applicants if they would be available to work on Sundays. If you're interviewing for a Monday to Friday, nine to five position you cannot.

Be very certain that you can directly tie each question you ask to some specific aspect of the position you're interviewing for.

4. Asking unnecessarily sensitive questions

We've already dealt with techniques for asking sensitive questions and indicated that sometimes it's necessary and even beneficial to delve into sensitive areas.

However, make sure that you're not delving unnecessarily. The position of interviewer is one of power and authority. As in any other situation where power is involved, it is tempting to seize the power and wield it.

Avoid the temptation. You're not interviewing to intimidate the applicants and demonstrate your authority. You're interviewing to determine whether or not each applicant fits the specific requirements of the position being filled.

Sensitive questions have their place and must be asked. Be careful, however, not to overdo it.

5. Not probing for depth

Inexperienced interviewers, especially, fall into this trap. They ask a question and, whether or not the response really gives them the information they need, they move on to the next question.

Don't be too timid to probe for the answers you're looking for. Don't be afraid to say, "Your answer really didn't get at the information I was looking for. Let me ask you again."

If the responses you get are superficial, you'll need to spend some time coaching and prompting the applicant to expand on the responses. But don't give up. This is your one chance to get the information you need.

e. WHAT QUESTIONS SHOULDN'T YOU ASK?

We've mentioned before that you should ask only those questions that pertain directly to the position you're trying to fill and that you need answers to in order to make an informed hiring choice.

Guidelines in both the United States and Canada specifically prohibit you from asking certain questions. Following is a list of potential interview questions. Place a check mark in the Yes column beside those questions you think you are legally allowed to ask in an interview, and a check mark in the No column beside those you believe you are not allowed to ask. Answers follow.

	Yes	No

1. Have you ever worked under a different name?
2. How many children do you have?
3. Will you start a family soon?
4. Would you be able to work on Saturdays to fulfill job requirements?
5. Can we see your birth certificate before we hire you?
6. Do you have any handicaps?
7. Were you born in this country?
8. What training did you receive in the army?
9. If you're hired, will you bring in a photograph for your personnel file?

10. Would you bring in a photograph to attach to your application?
11. Are you a U.S./Canadian citizen?
12. I see you attended St. Mark's High School. What kind of school is that?
13. Have your wages ever been garnisheed?
14. Who referred you for a position here?
15. That's an unusual name. What nationality is it?
16. Are you single, married, or divorced?
17. Do you plan to move any time soon?
18. This job requires a lot of heavy lifting. Do you have any physical problems we should know about?
19. You look like you had a North American ancestor. Am I right?
20. Do you own or rent your home?
21. What is your church affiliation?
22. Do you speak any languages fluently?
23. What schools have you attended?
24. Have you ever been arrested?
25. Who should we notify in case of an emergency?
26. Have you ever had trouble getting credit?
27. Will you include the name of your minister or pastor with your references?

Here are the answers. How well did you do?

1. Yes. You will need this information for the purpose of checking references.
2. No.
3. No.
4. Yes. Working Saturdays is a requirement of the job and you need to know the answer to this question.
5. No. You would have to ask for this information on the first day the applicant reported to work.
6. No.
7. No.
8. No, unless you are looking for specific, job-related training. If so, you should phrase your question to reflect this.
9. Yes. You can ask for a photo to be brought in *after* the candidate is hired.
10. No.
11. Yes.
12. No. This is a question that might be designed to determine religious background.
13. No.
14. Yes.
15. No.
16. No.
17. No.
18. Yes, because this requirement is directly related to the responsibilities of the job.
19. No.
20. No.
21. No.
22. Yes, if a job-related requirement.
23. Yes.
24. No. You may only ask about convictions, not arrests.
25. Yes.
26. No.
27. No. This question touches on religious affiliation.

You *cannot* ask any questions related to national origin; applicant's religion (name of church, minister, rabbi, etc.); religious holidays observed by the applicant; marital status or number of children; child care arrangements; where the applicant banks or the status of outstanding loans; whether the applicant rents or owns his or her place of residence; whether the applicant has ever served in the armed services of another country; or about any previous arrests.

Some of this information may be necessary for personnel records, but it can be obtained after the person has been hired and should have no bearing on hiring decisions.

Avoiding prohibited areas of questioning is not really as difficult as it may at first seem. A lot of your uncertainty can be relieved by putting each question through two tests:

(a) Does this question require an answer that would delve into a protected area (race, sex, religion, nationality, disability)?

(b) Do I need to know the answer to this question to make a hiring decision? Does the question relate directly to a requirement of the job?

If you answer no to (a) and yes to (b), you can be confident that you are asking a question that is permissible.

One special area of caution concerns pre-interview inquiries. During the first few minutes of meeting an applicant, when you are making "small talk" in an attempt to put the applicant at ease, you must be particularly on guard about what you say. If you ask, "Do you have children?" at this time it is just as illegal as it is when you get into the actual interview. (See chapter 10 for more information.)

f. CORE QUESTIONS

Much of the information you are looking for in interviews is the same whether you're hiring a mechanic or a vice-president. Below is a list of the 20 core questions that you will need to ask in any interview situation.

Before going over the "20 standards," however, one caution. As mentioned earlier, don't make the mistake of using the same set of questions, exactly as printed here, for every interview. You will want to personalize these standard questions to suit your company's hiring needs and your personal questioning style.

1. How did you become interested in this job?
2. In what ways is this line of work fulfilling to you?
3. Why do you feel you are qualified for this position?
4. What do you feel are the qualities of an ideal supervisor?
5. What personal qualities do you have that you feel would make you a good employee?
6. What did you find most (least) satisfying about your last job?
7. What do you enjoy doing in your free time?
8. What are your personal strengths (weaknesses)?
9. What are you doing to overcome your weaknesses?
10. What type(s) of people upset you? How do you deal with them?
11. Can you give me some examples of things you've done in previous jobs that demonstrate your willingness to work hard?
12. In what ways do you feel your fellow employees would find you an easy person to work with?
13. If you could relive your life, what changes would you make and what things would you do differently?
14. What were your favorite (least favorite) subjects in school?
15. How have you changed in the last three years?
16. In terms of your professional future, where do you see yourself five years from now?
17. What specific skills do you have to offer our company?

18. How do you deal with stress?
19. Do you enjoy working more with people or with things? Why?
20. Are there any additional aspects of your qualifications that I have not covered that you feel would be relevant to the position we are discussing?

7

CHECKING REFERENCES

A good employee is hard to find. So, in many cases, is a good reference. But, if you want to find good employees, you're going to have to do everything you can to assure yourself and others involved in the hiring decision that you are receiving good references.

a. WHY REFERENCE CHECKS ARE IMPORTANT

Ninety percent of all hiring mistakes can be prevented through proper reference checking procedures. Unfortunately, countless employers neglect to take this very important step in the hiring process. They rely, instead, on their own impression of the candidate based on resume, application, and interview.

This is a major mistake, and it can be a costly one. Checking the references of the applicants applying for a position is absolutely essential in obtaining accurate information about candidates' qualifications and experience.

It is estimated that approximately one-third of all job applicants either "lie" on their resumes and applications, or misrepresent their accomplishments.

You can see, then, why you need to add this important step to your hiring procedures.

b. PROBLEMS ALONG THE WAY

If so many employers fail to contact references of prospective employees there must be a good reason, right?

Well, there is. In fact, there are several good reasons. First, increasing numbers of lawsuits have caused former employers and personnel departments to be very cautious about giving out information on former employees. Many companies have policies that expressly prohibit the release of employee information other than name, title, and length of employment.

Second, references often have built-in biases which can be either positive or negative. It's difficult to evaluate the responses you receive to determine if the reference is providing you with objective information or biased, personal opinions.

Third, reference checking can be time-consuming. There is a tendency to want to hurry things along and make a decision, particularly when references are checked after the interview has been conducted. This is the point at which many employers decide to rely on "gut instinct."

Finally, reference checks require as much skill in questioning techniques as selection interviews. It's easy to fall into the trap of asking closed-ended questions that don't elicit the full response you need, or backing off when former employers seem reluctant to provide additional information.

c. WHEN AND WHO TO CONTACT

1. When to contact

Many employers call references *after* interviews have been conducted. This isn't necessarily the best procedure. Some employers find that, by calling references before scheduling the interview, they're able to more effectively screen out undesirable candidates, thus saving themselves the time they would have spent in an interview.

In addition, checking references before the interview can provide you with additional areas to explore during the interview and let you formulate pertinent questions in advance.

2. Who to contact

You should always seek permission from the job applicant before checking references. A good method of doing this is to ask, "Are there any former employers, co-workers, supervisors, or personal references that you would *not* want me to contact?" By phrasing the question in this way you leave yourself a lot of room to explore potential reference sources.

One of the reasons for leaving yourself latitude in this area is to give yourself the ability to network with the references you contact. For instance, suppose you call a former supervisor of a potential employee. During your conversation, the supervisor mentions the name of another supervisor in the organization who has previously managed this employee and who might be able to provide you with additional insight. You are then able to contact this person (providing it's not somebody who the candidate didn't want you to contact) without going back to the candidate to specifically ask, "Can I contact Joe Smith for a reference?"

Networking is an important aspect of reference checking and one you will want to make full use of. You will want to speak, if possible, to supervisors, co-workers, clients, or customers who are familiar with the person you're considering.

You should ask everybody you talk to if they could give you the name of somebody else in the firm who would be familiar with the applicant's qualifications and work performance.

An area of checking references that is frequently touchy is the current employer. Many job candidates do not want their current employer to know they are looking for work elsewhere. While you want to respect the wishes of these applicants, you're also aware that a current employer can provide you with perhaps the best insight into the applicant's qualifications and experience. To get around this problem, let the applicant know that if you make a firm offer of employment it will be contingent on receiving a satisfactory reference from his or her current employer. You reserve your right to withdraw the offer of employment if a satisfactory reference is not received.

Not only will this strategy help you get around the problem of not being able to contact a current employer, but it tends to encourage the applicant to be truthful with responses, since he or she knows that both the potential and the current position could be at risk.

3. Who not to contact

Invariably, the people who apply for positions with your company are going to provide you with a list of personal references and, possibly, letters of recommendation.

Give very little weight to these sources. Personal references will almost undoubtedly provide positive, even glowing, recommendations of the job applicant. The applicant is not going to include the names of people who would provide negative references.

Have you ever been handed a negative letter of recommendation by a job applicant? It's highly unlikely. It's not unlikely, however, for an applicant to provide you with a letter of recommendation that was written not by a reference, but by the applicant.

References from prominent members of an applicant's community are also often provided. Be extremely cautious about asking for or using a reference provided by a member of the clergy. This is an area that could get you into trouble for violation of equal employment opportunity regulations.

d. METHODS OF CHECKING REFERENCES

There are three ways to check references: in person, by mail, or by phone. We'll take a look at each of these methods, with an emphasis on telephone reference checks.

1. Checking references in person

While person-to-person reference checking is the most effective means of obtaining information about applicants, it is the least practical. If possible, however, there are several advantages to be gained from face-to-face meetings with an applicant's former employers and co-workers.

In a face-to-face meeting you will be able to judge non-verbal reactions of the people you are talking to. You'll find that people tend to be much more candid when you're sitting in the same room than if you were speaking on the phone or asking for written information.

Also, in a face-to-face meeting you'll have the advantage of meeting an applicant's former employer and being able to form your own judgments about the kind of supervisor this person would be. This sort of firsthand information will help you evaluate the candidate's responses to such questions as "What kind of supervisor do you get along best with?" or "What are some of the things you dislike in an employer?"

2. Checking references by mail

Mail is the least productive means of obtaining reference information, for three reasons:

(a) It can be a very slow process. You have no way of knowing if your letter was received by the right person and you cannot be assured of a quick response even if your questionnaire did fall into the right hands.

(b) Former employers are twice as unlikely to put their thoughts about former employees on paper as they are to tell you what they think in person or over the phone.

(c) Many people feel that filling out forms, of any kind, is a time-consuming imposition. They simply won't do it — and you won't have a reference.

If you do decide to contact references by mail, you should have a written form that quickly and adequately solicits the type of information you need.

3. Checking references by telephone

Reference checking by telephone is the most common means of obtaining information about job applicants. It is also a very effective means, because it is immediate, providing you reach the person you need right away; it is relatively inexpensive, especially when compared to reference checking in person; and it is possible to pick up on voice cues over the telephone which, though not as helpful as nonverbal body language, can still provide you with clues to the speaker's feelings.

(a) How to begin

When you make your initial contact with a reference, begin on a neutral note. It's often helpful to say something like, "I'm considering John Doe for employment and I'm calling to verify some information," rather than "I'm calling for a reference on John Doe."

The initial questions you ask should be nonthreatening and designed to simply verify factual information that has been provided in the resume or on the application form. You might want to ask about things such as the candidate's job title, the length of time the candidate was with the company, and the responsibilities required by the position the candidate held.

Be sure that you're speaking to somebody who has direct knowledge of the applicant's performance. It's not at all unusual to be routed to the personnel department where you will speak with someone who will provide you with the basic information on the candidate and little else.

(b) Using a structured reference guide

It's very important to be prepared when you place a call to a reference. One way of assuring that you will be prepared is by using a telephone reference check form like the one in Sample #7.

By using a telephone reference check form, you are able to conduct an efficient and continuous conversation with each reference you contact. You'll have the key questions at your fingertips and will be more likely to get accurate, objective information.

One caution, however: do be flexible in your approach. Don't feel that you are tied to the questions as they appear on the form. Keep in mind that the telephone reference check is really another form of interview and that you need to be open to the idea of pursuing avenues of questioning that you had not originally anticipated.

(c) Overcoming resistance

As was already mentioned earlier in this chapter, many employers will be very hesitant to provide anything but the bare facts about former (or current) employees. As a

SAMPLE #7
TELEPHONE REFERENCE CHECK

Applicant _____ Person contacted _____

Company called _____ Title _____

1. Was applicant employed by your company? Yes _____ No _____

2. What were the dates of employment? From _____ To _____

3. What was the job title? _____

4. What was the nature of the work performed? _____
    _____
    _____
    _____

5. Were there any promotions? Yes _____ No _____

    If yes, please describe circumstances _____
    _____

6. Applicant said he or she was earning $ _____ per _____ when leaving
    your company. Is this correct? Yes _____ No _____

7. Did applicant follow instructions satisfactorily? Yes _____ No _____

8. Did applicant lose any time at work because of poor health?
    No _____ Yes _____ Explain _____

9. How would you rate attendance? _____

10. What were this person's reasons for leaving your company? _____
    _____

11. Would you rehire? Yes _____ No _____ If not, why? _____
    _____

ADDITIONAL COMMENTS:

Date   Interviewer

_____   _____

potential new employer, however, you need to be persistent in order to overcome this reluctance. Here are some tips that can help you break through those barriers:

- Be confident in your approach.
- Begin the call in a neutral way, starting out with questions about factual aspects of the candidate's employment.
- Assure the reference that everything covered in the conversation will be strictly confidential.
- Stress the fact that you need this information to give the applicant fair consideration and that unless you're able to verify the information you've received, the candidate will not be considered for the position.
- If necessary, ask to speak to somebody at a higher level of management.

During all of your telephone or in-person reference checks, remember to listen carefully for not only what is said, but how it is said. Note any signs of hesitation, especially when you ask that crucial question, "Would you rehire this person?"

e. THE STANDARD QUESTION LIST

Many of the techniques and strategies you used in developing and conducting the selection interview (see chapters 4 and 5) can also be used in your reference checking. Again, the two important things to remember are —

(a) ask open-ended questions, and

(b) don't be afraid to probe for more detailed responses.

Here, then, are some of the most commonly asked questions for reference checking:

1. What were the applicant's specific dates of employment?
2. What was the applicant's job title?
3. How was the applicant's attendance record?
4. What were the applicant's initial/final responsibilities in this position?

5. How much supervision did the applicant require?
6. What were some of the applicant's strengths/ weaknesses?
7. How did the applicant compare to others who have held this same position?
8. Why did the applicant leave your organization?
9. What type of work-related conflicts did the applicant have?
10. What was the applicant's overall attitude to this position and his or her responsibilities in general?
11. What kinds of special contributions did the applicant make to your organization while employed by you?
12. Did the applicant work best independently or as part of a team?
13. Given the qualifications of the position, would you recommend that I hire this person?

And, finally, the most important question:

14. Would you rehire this person?

8

NARROWING IT DOWN
AND MAKING YOUR SELECTION

A recent nationwide study revealed that the last person
interviewed for a job is three times more likely to be hired
than the first person interviewed. Unfortunately, the last
person is not necessarily the best person. You can see why
it's important to establish an objective system for making a
hiring selection.

Remember the selection grid you prepared in chapter 3
to evaluate applicants? You'll find the same sort of form
helpful now as you narrow the candidates down to one
person who will be offered the job.

a. COMMON SELECTION MEASURES

On what evidence will you base your decision? There are
three commonly used selection measures that employers
use to evaluate job applicants. You may decide to use one or
a combination of all three. They are applicant self-report,
direct observation, and work samples.

1. Self-report

Self-report is the most commonly used selection measure.
An applicant comes to an interview and tells the prospective employer about his or her accomplishments and experience. This is the method discussed in previous chapters.

This is, obviously, a very biased means of learning about
the candidate. As was true with resumes, an applicant is
unlikely to provide you with negative information about
his or her accomplishments.

Since this is a commonly used evaluation measure, however, it's important for employers to realize the limitations

involved and, whenever possible, to combine this measure with one of the other two.

2. Direct observation

If you can directly observe a job applicant performing a representative job task, you will be in a much better position to evaluate job potential.

Unfortunately, direct observation is not always possible. How would you, for instance, observe a managerial candidate making a decision? And you don't want to put an untried job candidate in a position to affect your company's product, productivity, or credibility. You don't, for instance, ask applicants for a receptionist position to answer the phones for a while so you can observe their competence.

There are, however, ways to get around this problem:

(a) You can use one of the tests that have been developed to measure analytical and decision-making ability. One well-known test is the "in-basket" exercise, which gives the interviewee a certain amount of time to examine the contents of a simulated in-basket, analyze each problem, and determine what action to take. During this test the applicant is carefully observed and judged on organization and problem-solving abilities.

(b) Some tasks can be role-played. With the receptionist position, for example, you might develop some scenarios that you could play out with each applicant to evaluate his or her responses.

(c) You can use hypothetical questions or situations to approximate real-life situations. You might present a job candidate with a problem and ask him or her to tell you the steps to be taken to solve the problem.

(d) Some tasks can be directly observed. For instance, you could ask a clerical applicant to file invoices or type a letter, an applicant for an editorial position to edit a page of copy, etc.

If you find that direct observation would be virtually impossible, you may still be able to take a look at work samples.

3. Work samples

Artistic positions, especially, lend themselves to the use of work samples in applicant evaluation. Graphic designers, for example, might be asked to bring in samples of their design work. A technical writer might be asked to bring in writing samples.

b. COMMON SELECTION CRITERIA

The job specifications you set up in chapter 1 before you even started looking for potential applicants should be foremost in your mind as you start to narrow down the choice of job applicants.

Applicants should be evaluated both in terms of how well they meet the job specifications and how they compare to other applicants. For this reason it is important to reserve a final decision until all interviews have been completed. Don't make a yes or no decision after each interview. It is better to wait until all interviews are completed and then rate interviewees on the basis of the criteria you have determined are the best predictors of job performance.

The criteria you use will not necessarily be the same as the criteria another employer might use. There are individual differences based on the qualifications necessary to perform the particular job, the company's historical hiring practices, and the value the company places on certain individual attributes.

Some common selection criteria are intelligence, communication skills, self-confidence, sociability, ambition and motivation, leadership, adaptability, and cooperativeness. These criteria are behavioral traits that you must assess throughout the interview based on your impressions of the candidate.

Sample #8 is an example of an interview summary form that would typically be filled out after each interview. Later, these forms prove useful as you compare the candidates and rank them in terms of their ability to meet the requirements of the job.

At this time, you may want to go back and use the selection grid (see Sample #6) to clearly compare job candidates.

c. RATING ERRORS

In any evaluation process there is a possibility for error. Following are some typical rating errors and suggestions for how to avoid letting these errors influence your hiring decisions.

1. Typical rating errors

(a) Halo effect

A halo effect refers to a person's tendency to rate all aspects of performance based on the observance of one trait. For instance, if you observe that a certain candidate is a very articulate and enthusiastic communicator, you might rate this candidate high on all characteristics.

(b) Horn effect

The opposite of the halo effect, the horn effect refers to the tendency to let one poor rating influence all other ratings, resulting in a lower overall evaluation than is really deserved.

(c) Error of central tendency

The error of central tendency describes the clustering of appraisals around a central point — usually an average or middle point on a scale. This is both the most common and most serious type of error. It can result from the fear of rating too high or too low; it may seem safer to cluster all scores toward the center to avoid the appearance of bias when evaluating candidates.

(d) Stereotyping or initial impression

Because stereotypes may be subconscious, we may often be unfairly biased without being aware of it. First impressions really do make lasting impressions. It is extremely important to base any evaluation on observable, objective behaviors rather than subjective opinions.

SAMPLE #8
INTERVIEW SUMMARY

POSITION FOR WHICH INDIVIDUAL IS BEING CONSIDERED: _____

NAME OF INDIVIDUAL BEING INTERVIEWED: _____

DEPARTMENT: _____ INTERVIEW DATE: _____

INSTRUCTIONS: RATE THE APPLICANT BY PLACING AN "X" IN THE APPROPRIATE
BOX FOR EACH CATEGORY.

APPEARANCE	SLOPPY, UNTIDY OR FAULTY GROOMING		GENERALLY NEAT WELL-GROOMED		VERY CAREFUL OF APPEARANCE METICULOUS IN DRESS
POISE	ILL AT EASE, TENSE EMBARRASSED, AWKWARD		COMPOSED, RELAXED, COMFORTABLE		ENTIRELY AT EASE, SPONTANEOUS, POLISHED
CONVERSATIONAL ABILITY	DISORGANIZED, CONFUSED, WANDERS, IRRELEVANT, EVASIVE		LOGICAL AND CLEAR, GRAMMAR GOOD, ORGANIZED, RELEVANT		ANIMATED, FLUENT, GOOD VOCABULARY
ALERTNESS	SLOW TO RESPOND: DOESN'T SEEM TO UNDERSTAND		COMPREHENDS QUICKLY, RESPONDS READILY		SHARP, KEEN, PERCEPTIVE
LIKABILITY	COLD, ALOOF, SNOBBISH COCKY, UNFRIENDLY		PLEASANT, AMIABLE, INGRATIATING		EXCEPTIONALLY PERSONABLE, CHARMING, ATTRACTIVE PERSONALITY
ENTHUSIASM	FAILS TO GIVE IMPRESSION OF SINCERE INTEREST IN JOB		PLENTY OF DRIVE, HAS PLANS FOR GETTING AHEAD, IS EXCITED ABOUT JOB		EXTREMELY WELL-MOTIVATED FOR JOB AND FUTURE WITH THE COMPANY
INITIATIVE	RARELY VOLUNTEERS INFORMATON OR TAKES THE LEAD		SEIZES OPPORTUNITY TO ENLARGE RESPONSES		WELL-ORGANIZED PRESENTATION ANTICIPATES QUESTIONS, ASKS GOOD QUESTIONS
JOB-RELATED EDUCATION	WEAK		GOOD		EXCEPTIONAL
JOB-RELATED EXPERIENCE	LACKING		BASICALLY QUALIFIED		WELL QUALIFIED

Summarize your conclusions about this individual, giving specific reasons and paying particular attention to the experience and competence of the individual as it relates to the particular job requirements of
the position to be filled.

Based on your interview, do you recommend filling the vacancy with this applicant?

                                                      YES   NO

If yes, did you get applicant's permission to contact present employer in our reference check procedures?   **YES   NO**

_____

Signature of Person conducting the Interview

DISPOSITION:

(e) Projection or similarity error

An error of projection or similarity is reflected in the saying, "Birds of a feather flock together." It's easy to recognize that we tend to like people who are like us and to dislike people who are unlike us. This can become a problem in the rating process when you give high scores to applicants because they either consciously or unconsciously "remind me of myself when I was just starting out," or low scores to another applicant who "just doesn't have the ambition that I have."

(f) Interindividual error

This error consists of basing each applicant's evaluation on a comparison with other applicants. This is why it is very important to make a final decision at the end of all the interviews rather than after each applicant leaves your office.

2. Steps to error-free evaluations

The evaluation process, by its very nature, is quite subjective, leaving many areas open to bias and error. Your awareness of the possibility of errors occurring is one of the first steps to becoming a fair evaluator of job applicants.

The checklist below can help make this demanding task a little easier.

(a) Be prepared.

(b) Identify desired behaviors in observable rather than subjective terms.

(c) Be aware of your own personal biases and work to overcome them.

(d) Try using more than one interviewer and comparing results to determine possible bias.

(e) Don't assume that excellence in one area implies excellence in all areas.

(f) Base judgments on *demonstrated* performance, not *anticipated* performance.

(g) Base judgments on observable standards, not on a comparison with other applicants.

d. MAKING THE OFFER

If you have religiously followed all the steps outlined up to this point, you should feel confident in the choice you've made. The next step is to extend an offer.

You may decide to extend an offer by mail, by phone, or in person. Two important things to remember are —

(a) try to make the offer as soon as possible after the interview, and

(b) be sure to provide all the facts associated with the offer (e.g., salary, terms of relocation, benefits, starting date), and any other information that might influence the prospective employee's decision of whether or not to take the job.

9

THE TEN MOST COMMON MISTAKES MADE IN EMPLOYEE SELECTION

On March 1 you began interviews for an assistant. On March 3 you hired the first person you interviewed. She didn't exactly have the qualifications you'd been looking for, but had been sympathetic to your lack of time to prepare for the meeting. You had immediately recognized her as an outgoing, hardworking individual — much like yourself. Most of the interview had been spent comparing various interests, with you doing most of the talking. Your most probing question was "You don't mind working overtime, do you?" Of course she said "no," and your decision was made. The other candidates looked pale in comparison, and you offered her the position.

On April 1, her first day of work, she was late. The second day she called in sick. The third day she just didn't show up. And, after putting up with her for the past six working days, you wish she'd stay home more often.

What went wrong?

Several things. In fact, in the course of your hiring procedure you made every one of the ten most common mistakes in employee selection. They are listed below:

(a) Inadequate screening
(b) Inadequate preparation for the interview
(c) Lack of knowledge of the position to be filled
(d) Unintentional coaching
(e) Ineffective use of questions
(f) Dominating the interview
(g) Stereotyping the candidate
(h) Failure to probe for depth
(i) Evaluating solely in relation to other candidates

(j) Premature evaluation and selection

Let's take a closer look at each of these.

a. INADEQUATE SCREENING

You've advertised for an employee and your desk is piled high with applications. What do you do now?

The first thing you need to do — something you should have done before you ever advertised for help — is to determine the specifications for the job. What skills and qualifications does the applicant absolutely have to have? Set up your specifications before you ever look at the applications so there is no chance that you'll be fooled by impressive though unsuitable resumes.

Now, establish a checklist. Go through each resume, automatically disqualifying those that don't meet your specifications.

Don't be swayed by applicants who write persuasively, who call or visit your office to ask more about the job, who dwell on their on-the-job experience and ignore your educational requirements, or who ignore your request for experience but try to convince you that their extensive education is experience enough.

Some of the questions you should be asking yourself about the position include —

- What is the primary reason for the job?
- What is difficult about the job?
- How much supervision is provided?
- What types of people must the new employee get along with?
- What technical knowledge or experience is required?
- Will the position you have open be a challenge to the applicant? Too much of a challenge?

In terms of individual applicants you need to ask —

- What is the work history of the applicant?
- How often has the applicant changed jobs? Why?
- Has the applicant progressed in past positions?

- Is the applicant's education appropriate to the job?

The number of qualified applicants per hundred responses is very low. Most hiring consultants suggest that you try to weed out the applications and limit your interview list to a maximum of five candidates.

b. INADEQUATE PREPARATION

If you set up an interview and immediately proceed to ask the applicant questions that he or she has already answered in the resume, you're not prepared. You're wasting your time, your company's time, and the applicant's time. After the interview is over you'll sit at your desk with no better idea of how qualified the applicant is than when you read the letter of application.

Before you begin the interview you need to determine the job requirements, thoroughly examine the resume or application, plan and organize pertinent interview questions, and arrange to have a private place to conduct the interview.

The three major errors are failure to read appropriate materials before the interview, failure to develop questioning strategy, and inadequate knowledge of the position.

c. LACK OF KNOWLEDGE OF THE POSITION TO BE FILLED

The manager of the position is usually the only person who knows the requirements well enough to make an accurate, in-depth assessment of a candidate's qualifications.

You need to know exactly what the candidate will need in terms of experience, education, knowledge and skills, characteristics/attitudes, interpersonal skills. You also need to know what the candidate wants in terms of salary, relocation help, availability, and travel.

Lack of relevant job information will increase the chances of your making the wrong choice by using the wrong standards.

d. UNINTENTIONAL COACHING

Sometimes, without meaning to, you may find yourself asking leading questions. You may not even realize that you're doing this. Leading interviewees to a response can be a major problem, since you will not know if you are obtaining accurate information or whether the responses have been influenced by the tone of your voice, your body language, etc.

One major coaching mistake that is made almost universally, and that can be easily corrected, is telling the applicant about the job and its requirements before you do the interview. You should wait until all your questions have been answered before "tipping off" the job candidate in this way.

Another problem is the use of leading questions such as "This position involves a great deal of stress — how well do you handle stress?" The applicant immediately knows that to answer this question correctly, he or she should say that she deals with stress positively.

As an interviewer you need to make a nonbiased choice. To do this effectively, be sure to guard against asking leading questions.

e. INEFFECTIVE USE OF QUESTIONS

As discussed in chapter 6, there are five types of interview questions and each has a specific purpose. You should know when and why to use each of these question types. Here is a quick review:

(a) Open-ended questions are meant to get the applicant to expand on a topic by providing more than a simple yes or no answer. An example might be "Why did you decide to apply for this position?"

(b) Closed-ended questions allow for only a yes or no response. While open-ended questions are generally preferred, the closed-ended question does have its place. Closed-ended questions are useful for getting specific answers. The responses to these questions can be easily tabulated and compared between applicants. For example, "Do you mind working overtime?" or "How long did you work at XYZ Company?" can provide you with an easy means of comparing several applicants.

(c) Leading questions should be avoided. You don't want to be guiding the applicants' responses by implying what the answers should be. Leading questions have a low potential for generating truthful responses. Examples of leading questions are "You do enjoy working with numbers, don't you?" or "I'm sure you wouldn't mind working late some evenings, would you?"

(d) Sensitive questions allow you to explore delicate issues in a nonthreatening way. There are certain answers that you must have to make a hiring choice; sometimes these answers require carefully worded questions. For instance, you need to know why an applicant left his or her last job. You might begin your inquiry by saying, "There are any number of reasons why a person decides to look for new employment. Could you tell me why you decided to leave your position with XYZ Company to seek employment elsewhere?" Begin your question by legitimizing the response. Let your applicant know that you are not sitting in judgment, but that you need to ask certain questions that might be considered delicate.

(e) Hypothetical questions can be the most helpful to you in the search for a new employee. With this type of question, you are not necessarily looking for a specific answer; you're trying, in most cases, to explore the applicant's problem-solving and decision-making skills. An example of a hypothetical question might be "Suppose you're the kind of person who likes to be very organized and, every night before you leave the office, you make a list of things to do the next day. But, when you come in one morning, several people approach you with projects they say are urgent and need to be done immediately. What do you do?" Base your hypothetical question on the job you're filling. This can be a good way of determining if an applicant would fit the job.

f. DOMINATING THE INTERVIEW

Domination can result from failing to be prepared, nervousness, or not knowing when to stop talking. You'll learn nothing about the job applicant if you do all the talking. Your job is to create an atmosphere that will encourage the applicant to talk. You must learn to lead the discussion but not dominate it.

Be on guard for the following listening problems:
- Accepting the presence of unnecessary distractions
- Being preoccupied with yourself
- Expecting to be bored, bothered, or turned off
- Making before-the-fact judgments about the person speaking
- Competing with the interviewee to control the conversation
- Selective listening — only hearing what you expect to hear

A good rule of thumb is that the applicant should be talking about 70% of the time.

g. STEREOTYPING THE CANDIDATE

First impressions are hard to forget. In fact, we have all come to recognize the phrase "Make your first impression count" as what it is — a truism.

As an interviewer, however, you have to watch yourself very carefully so that you don't fall into the trap of stereotyping the job applicants. You may have predetermined what the ideal candidate will be like. You may even have a picture in your head of what the successful candidate will look like. But the candidates that fit your picture may not necessarily be the best candidates for the job.

In particular, you should watch out for the following:

1. The likable candidate

Some people are naturally vivacious and charming. You like them immediately. But you don't have to like the people who you hire; you only have to like their work.

If you find yourself in an interview with an extremely likable person, enjoy the interview, but remain objective when you begin the selection process for the job.

2. The mirror image

We naturally tend to like people who are most like ourselves. This holds true in the business world as well as in our personal relationships.

Be aware of this tendency when you are conducting interviews. A candidate who attended the same school you did, who shares your political views, and who is near your age is not necessarily the most qualified person for the job.

3. The poised applicant

Some applicants are poised and self-confident. They present themselves well. Others are nervous and ill at ease. They shift in their chairs, answer your questions in one-syllable monotones, and end up making you feel miserable by the time the interview is over.

Nervous people are not necessarily bad choices. If you're looking for a salesperson you may have good reason for not wanting to hire a wallflower, but for many other jobs you may be cheating yourself if you immediately disqualify the nervous applicants.

There are many possible stereotypes. You should be aware of your own biases before you begin interviewing. And if you find yourself in an interview with someone who brings out your biases for some reason, make an effort to be objective — for yourself, for the company, but particularly for the applicant.

h. FAILURE TO PROBE FOR DEPTH

Many interviewers, particularly those with little experience, will accept inadequate responses to questions. They will accept superficial or ambiguous answers, fail to ask for clarification, and make incorrect assumptions.

Here are some examples of probing statements you should use when you don't feel a question has been answered thoroughly enough:

"Could you explain what you meant by . . .?"

"Tell me more about that."

"How did you feel about that?"

It can be difficult to press for answers to questions that you sense are sensitive. However, the answers to these questions can be vitally important to your hiring decision. Candidates at interviews know they will be asked some tough questions. Don't back down. If you need to know, you need to ask.

i. EVALUATING SOLELY IN RELATION TO OTHER CANDIDATES

Consider the following scenario: The first person you interview doesn't really have all the right qualifications and doesn't really meet the specifications you've established, but somehow you just hit it off together. You spend most of the interview talking about mutual interests, and you can really "tell" that this person has a "feel" for the job. You've got your mind made up — this is the person you're going to hire.

During the rest of the interviews you are preoccupied, and when you do pay attention to what the other applicants are saying you compare them to the first applicant so that you can legitimize your decision.

You need to rate *all* the interviewees on the basis of the criteria you established before you began the interviews.

When your first interview goes well — the questions are answered smoothly and the candidate is at ease — there is a tendency for remaining candidates to lose points in comparison.

Objectivity is the most important factor in evaluating all applicants. Go back to the standards you established and compare each and every applicant to these standards — not to each other. Resist the temptation to add new standards because some glib applicant touted qualifications you hadn't originally included in your specifications.

j. PREMATURE EVALUATION AND SELECTION

You may be very good at not making judgments about the people you have interviewed until all the interviews are over. Or you may be like most other interviewers and make a decision after each person leaves your office.

First impressions can be inaccurate and are assuredly incomplete. When you rely on subjective hunches, or let yourself make premature decisions, you risk the possibility of creating a self-fulfilling prophecy. The applicants who look good on initial impressions will automatically appear to be the best candidates; the "bad" applicants will automatically appear poor candidates.

You should not make any decisions until all interviews have been completed. Many interviewers make the mistake of automatically weeding applicants immediately after the interview is over — sometimes even sooner. Resist the impulse to do this.

Keep an open mind. Make no decision until you have interviewed all applicants.

10
AVOIDING LEGAL LIABILITY

Tami is 22 and has spent the past two months actively looking for a full-time job where she can put her recently acquired business degree to use. On two occasions she has been involved in a one-to-one interview with a potential employer who preceded the "serious" questioning with some "background" information. For example —

"Are you married?"

"Do you plan to marry?"

"What about children?"

Denise works for her local municipality as a light equipment operator. Recently, a position was posted for a heavy equipment operator. As she was signing her name, a supervisor from the department with the job opening came up behind her. Chuckling, he patted her on the back. "What's a little thing like you thinking of a position like this for, honey? We need a big, brawny man to handle this job."

These two situations are fictitious, but this type of activity happens every day to thousands of people across the country. Aren't these things illegal? You bet. And, as an employer, you'd better be certain that your hiring practices don't include this type of blatant discriminatory practice —or even less blatant, but equally illegal, actions.

a. GUIDELINES IN CANADA

All jurisdictions in Canada have legislation designed to ensure the equality of its people. These statutes have their origin in the 1948 Universal Declaration of Human Rights (UDHR) of the United Nations. All jurisdictions express opposition to discrimination on the basis of race, nationality, ethnic origin or place of origin, color, religion or creed, marital status, or sex. Table #2 indicates, by jurisdiction, the prohibited grounds of discrimination.

TABLE #2
PROHIBITED GROUNDS OF DISCRIMINATION
(Canada)

Jurisdiction	Dependence on alcohol/drug	Race	National/ethnic origin	Color	Nationality/citizenship	Religion	Age	Sex	Pregnancy/childbirth*	Marital status	Criminal conviction	Mental handicap
Federal	•	•	•	•		•	•	•	•	•	•	•
Alberta		•		•		•	• (18+)	•	•	•		
British Columbia		•		•		•	• (45-65)	•		•	•	•
Manitoba		•	•	•	•	•	•	•	/	•		•
New Brunswick		•	•	•		•	• (19+)	•		•		•
Newfoundland		•	•	•		•	• (19-65)	•		•		•
Nova Scotia		•	•	•		•	• (40-65)	•		•		
Ontario		•	•	•	•	•	• (18-65)	•		•	•	•
Prince Edward Island		•	•	•		•	•	•		•		•
Quebec		•	•	•		•	•	•	•	•	•	•
Saskatchewan		•	•	•	•	•	• (18-65)	•		•		
Northwest Territories		•		•	•		•	•		•	•	•
Yukon Territory		•	•	•		•		•		•		

*In Alberta discrimination on the basis of pregnancy is deemed to be discrimination on the basis of sex.
**Harassment is banned on all proscribed grounds of discrimination.

98

TABLE #2 — Continued

Physical handicap	Ancestry	Political belief	Family status	Sexual orientation	Harassment**	Civil status	Language	Source of income	Social origin	Social conditions	Creed	Place of residence	Place of origin
•			•		•								
•	•										•		•
•	•	•											•
•		•	•					•					
•	•												•
•		•			•				•		•		
•								•			•		
•	•		•		•						•		•
•		•									•		
•		•		•	•	•	•		•	•			
•	•										•		•
•	•			•							•	•	•
	•										•		

99

The authority to enact laws in Canada is divided between the provincial and the federal governments. The laws enacted by the federal government are contained in the Canada Labour Code, and apply mainly to employees of federal Crown corporations and federally regulated areas such as broadcasting, including the following:

(a) Works or undertakings connecting a province with another province or country, such as railways, bus operations, trucking, pipelines, ferries, tunnels, bridges, canals, and telegraph and cable systems

(b) All extra-provincial shipping and services connected with such shipping (e.g., longshoring and stevedoring)

(c) Air transport, aircraft and aerodromes

(d) Radio and television broadcasting

(e) Banks

(f) Defined operations of specific works that have been declared to be for the general advantage of Canada or of two or more provinces, such as flour, feed and seed cleaning mills, feed warehouses, grain elevators, the British Columbia Telephone Company, and uranium mining and processing

(g) Most federal Crown corporations (e.g., the Canadian Broadcasting Corporation and the St. Lawrence Seaway Authority)

The Canadian Human Rights Act regulates discrimination against employees who come under federal jurisdiction. Other employees are covered by the human rights codes of their provinces. For more information on employer/employee rights in your province, consult the appropriate Employee/Employer Rights Guide published by Self-Counsel Press.

1. Canadian Human Rights Act

The Canadian Human Rights Act prohibits discrimination on the grounds of race, national or ethnic origin, color, religion, age, sex, marital status, family status, disability, and conviction for which a pardon has been granted. The act further states that if a complaint is based on pregnancy or childbirth, the discrimination shall be deemed to be based on the ground of sex.

However, under the act it is not a discriminatory practice to —

(a) refuse, exclude, suspend, specify, or express a preference in relation to employment if based on a bona fide occupational requirement,

(b) refuse or terminate employment because an individual has not reached the minimum age for legal employment by law or under regulations,

(c) terminate an individual's employment because that person has reached normal retirement age for employees in similar positions,

(d) vest or lock in pension contributions if the terms and conditions of a pension fund or plan established by an employer provide for the compulsory vesting or locking in of pension contributions at a fixed or determinable age,

(e) discriminate on a prohibited ground of discrimination in a manner that is proscribed by guidelines issued by the Commission, or

(f) grant a female employee maternity leave.

2. The Canadian Human Rights Commission

The Commission consists of a chief commissioner and a deputy chief commissioner in addition to three to six members who may be either full- or part-time.

The Commission administers the Canadian Human Rights Act, the conduct of public information programs, the sponsorship of research projects, and the review of regulations and orders issued by parliament to determine whether they are consistent with the principles expressed in the Canadian Human Rights Act.

In addition to the Commission, a human rights tribunal panel has been established whose members are appointed by the Governor General.

3. Complaints

An individual or group of individuals may file a complaint within the Commission if there are reasonable grounds for believing that a person has engaged in or is engaging in a discriminatory practice. The discriminatory act or omission must have occurred —

(a) in Canada and the aggrieved person was lawfully present in Canada or, if absent, was entitled to return,

(b) outside Canada and the person discriminated against was a Canadian citizen or a person admitted for permanent residence, or

(c) in Canada and was a discriminatory practice against a class of individuals rather than one person in particular (e.g., discriminatory advertisements, discriminatory employment policies, and hate literature).

After the complaint has been filed, the Commission may request the president of the human rights tribunal panel to appoint a human rights tribunal to inquire into the complaint. As the result of such an inquiry, a person may be ordered to —

(a) cease the discriminatory practice and take measures to prevent a similar practice from occurring in the future, including the adoption of an affirmative action plan,

(b) make available the rights, opportunities, or privileges that were denied the victim as the result of the discriminatory practice, or

(c) compensate the victim for lost wages and any expenses incurred as a result of the discriminatory practice.

In Canada, as in the United States, the emphasis is on fair and consistent treatment of all potential and current employees. Common sense and fair dealings should prevail in any of your recruitment, interviewing, and selection procedures.

Take steps now to prevent problems from occurring. Make sure that your hiring practices are fair, equitable, and consistent.

b. GUIDELINES IN THE UNITED STATES

It is important to remember that it is the *consequence* of employment practices and not the *intent* that determines whether discrimination exists. Any employment practice or policy, regardless of how innocuous in intent, which has a "disparate effect" on members of a "protected class" constitutes unlawful discrimination unless it can be proven that such a policy is required due to "business necessity."

The Supreme Court has ordered the removal of "artificial, arbitrary and unnecessary barriers to employment when the barriers operate invidiously to discriminate on the basis of racial or other impermissible classification." These practices and policies may take place during recruitment, selection, placement, testing, transfer, promotion, seniority, lines of progression, and many other of the basic terms and conditions of employment.

The removal of these barriers requires positive affirmative action to provide new policies and practices. It also requires a firm knowledge of the rules and regulations surrounding equal employment opportunity and the affirmative action concept.

In the United States, affirmative action refers to equal opportunity in employment for all people regardless of physical handicap, race, nationality, age, sex, religion, or any other nonjob-related means of determining eligibility for a position of employment. It is a term that encompasses various methods through which the concept of equal employment opportunity becomes a reality.

1. Legislation prohibiting discrimination in employment

The affirmative action concept became law in 1964 with the enactment of the Civil Rights Act. Title VII mandates equal employment opportunity by —

(a) prohibiting job discrimination on the basis of race, color, religion, sex, or national origin, and

(b) establishing an Equal Employment Opportunity Commission (EEOC) to administer the law.

The EEOC is a five-member independent executive agency which is authorized to receive and investigate discrimination complaints filed by individuals and EEOC commissioners and to remedy any discriminatory practices encountered. If mediation and conciliation fail, the EEOC can file suit against private employers on behalf of the charging party. The Justice Department may file suit against public sector employers.

There are three ways in which allegations of discrimination may come to the EEOC:

(a) Individuals may file complaints.
(b) EEOC Commissioners may file on behalf of an individual. Class action suits may be filed against both the public and private sectors.

Penalties which may be imposed include the following:

(a) Cease and desist orders to stop all hiring
(b) Reimbursement of back pay
(c) Reinstatement of employees who have been terminated due to discrimination
(d) Institutional change in personnel systems
(e) Establishment of quota hiring systems
(f) Development of affirmative action plans
(g) Elimination of artificial barriers to employment which tend to screen out groups protected by Title VII of the Civil Rights Act of 1984

For employers, recognizing the possibility of bias in selection is the first step toward correcting the problem. Decision-makers should make efforts to quantitatively specify the work-related criteria that will be used in the selection process and then make their judgments based solely on these criteria.

2. Improving recruiting efforts

The EEOC has listed six major guidelines for employers to follow in establishing fair recruitment practices:

(a) Analyzing current recruitment procedures to eliminate such discriminatory barriers as word of mouth or walk-in sources of employees

(b) Establishing objective measures to monitor the applicant pool in the recruitment process (e.g., enabling the employer to identify how many candidates were females and/or minorities)

(c) Training recruiters so that they use only fair objectives and job-related criteria

(d) Maintaining files on minority and women applicants not hired for one job that may be used in future recruiting, and fully utilizing women and minorities who are already on the staff as recruiters, sources of information, and interviewers

(e) Publicizing vacancies by means of advertising directed toward recruiting as many minorities and women as possible, including the use of the suggested phrase, "Equal Opportunity Employer M/F" (Avoid references to age, sex, race, national origin, and marital status. Minimum qualifications needed to perform the job should be stated.)

(f) Making full use of community resources, including educational institutions, women's and minorities' organizations, employment services, and public training programs, and placing ads in newspapers that will be read by minority groups.

3. Fine-tuning the selection process

Discrimination in hiring practices does occur — as many find out to their dismay and frustration. The EEOC has found that the selection process itself contains more possibility for discrimination than any other area of hiring practice.

In an effort to deal with these problems the EEOC has set up guidelines which employers are expected to follow.

(a) Selection procedures must be based on job-related standards. Criteria used to select employees must be demonstrably related to job performance. Only when sex is a "bona fide occupational qualification" can it be used as a determinant in hiring.

(b) If discrimination in hiring is indicated, employers must be able to prove that they have, indeed, used valid hiring standards.

(c) Jobs cannot be classified by sex or any other discriminatory means. Nor can there be sex-based, separate lines of progression or seniority lists.

(d) Job opportunities must be advertised without indicating preference, limitation, specification, or discrimination because of sex or any other discriminatory measure unless there is a *bona fide occupational qualification* (BFOQ).

(e) In regard to pre-employment inquiries, all personnel involved in employment decisions are prohibited from asking questions that express a limitation, specification, or discrimination as to sex. An applicant may be asked to indicate his or her sex, provided the question is put in good faith that the information will not be used for discriminatory purposes.

4. Avoiding nonessential inquiries

When interviewing candidates for a position, ask yourself these questions:

- Does this question result in the screening out of women and minorities?
- Is this question necessary to judge competence in job performance?
- Are there other nondiscriminatory ways to obtain this information?

Court decisions and the EEOC have found many common preemployment inquiries to disproportionately reject minorities and females. Some of these questions have been expressly prohibited by the courts. These include questions referring to the following areas:

(a) Race, religion, and national origin

Though not expressly prohibited from recording this information in personnel files for affirmative action purposes, these inquiries are explicitly prohibited in many states. In the event of discrimination charges, information of this nature recorded in the personnel files will be examined very carefully.

(b) Education

Requirements for education that are not specifically needed for the job in question may be placed under examination in discrimination suits. Inflated education requirements can result in higher turnover due to overqualified employees and can serve to eliminate women and other minorities from the job force.

(c) Arrest and conviction records

These questions are unlawful as the basis for employment unless the employer can demonstrate a "business necessity."

(d) Sex, marital, and family status

The Supreme Court has ruled that an employer may not have different hiring practices for men and women with pre-school children. In addition, any questions related to marital or family status, if asked of female candidates, must also be asked of male candidates. This information is needed for Social Security and tax records, but it can be obtained after employment. Although many personnel officials may argue this point, studies have shown that there is little difference in the absenteeism of women when compared to that of men.

(e) Physical requirements

Requirements related to height, weight, etc., should be obtained when necessary for the performance of a particular job. An employer must be able to show that these requirements are reasonably related to job performance.

(f) Age

The Age Discrimination in Employment Act of 1967, amended in 1978, prohibits discrimination against workers between 40 and 70 years of age. Its stated purpose is "to promote the employment of older persons based on their ability rather than their age."

5. Maintenance of records

Even if you can honestly say that your employment methods are fair and you have never had any problems with grievances, you must still maintain records of your employment practices. This is necessary both to satisfy federal laws and to protect yourself in the event of a future grievance.

Under federal law, all recruitment forms must be retained for at least one year after an employment decision has been made. Under the Age Discrimination Act, employers must retain job applications of successful applicants for at least three years after they are hired.

11

ORIENTATION AND TRAINING

You've done it!

You've hired a new employee after weeks (or even months) of searching. You've advertised, screened resumes, searched through applications, prepared interview questions, asked the right questions, checked references, and made your final selection.

Before you can get this new person up and running, however, there is one more task to complete — employee orientation. The first prerequisite for maintaining an effective staff is hiring the right person. The second prerequisite is skillful employee orientation.

a. YOUR EXPECTATIONS FOR ORIENTATION AND TRAINING

Just as in the interview, you will come to the orientation session with certain expectations. You will expect to provide the employee with pertinent information about the company and its policies, determine the extent of the employee's training and experience as it relates to specific job duties, develop feelings of belonging and acceptance, and avoid creating unnecessary anxiety.

During the orientation period you also want to provide the employee with copies of the job description, job specifications, and job standards.

Your expectations for the orientation session can also be defined as goals. Later in this chapter we will look more specifically at how you can accomplish these goals in the orientation session.

b. THE EMPLOYEE'S EXPECTATIONS FOR ORIENTATION AND TRAINING

As in virtually every aspect of human relations, you and your new employee will differ somewhat in what you expect the orientation and initial training period to accomplish. This is a natural dichotomy. Each of you will come to this initial meeting with different hopes and fears.

The employee, of course, hopes to do a good job. The employee has another, perhaps even more important, expectation — that he or she will "fit in" by getting along well with supervisors and co-workers.

As an employer, your major hope is that the employee will succeed and, in essence, make you look good. After all, you were the person responsible for hiring and you are now the person responsible for training.

You can see, then, that while training the employee to do a good job is going to be important, your first goal should be to make the new employee feel comfortable by establishing a sense of belonging.

c. GUIDELINES FOR AN EFFECTIVE ORIENTATION

What can you do to make the orientation session successfully meet your training needs while minimizing anxiety for the employee?

Following are some guidelines that may prove helpful.

1. Welcome

Initially you should welcome the employee and reestablish the rapport that you had during your initial interview. Begin with some small talk and move slowly into the real business of the meeting. Acknowledge the fact that the employee may be uncomfortable and nervous and demonstrate your acceptance of these feelings.

Once you sense that your new employee is becoming more relaxed, you're ready to move into the information session that begins the orientation session.

2. Organization chart

It's important that the new employee understands the structure of the company and how his or her position fits into that structure. At the beginning of the orientation session you will want to show the new employee a copy of the organizational chart and explain how the departments and divisions are organized and how the new employee's department relates to others in the company. This is also the time to explain the chain of command in operation in your organization.

3. Company and department objectives

What are the goals of the company? The new employee will need to know the answer to this question to be able to understand how he or she can contribute to these objectives.

What is the reason for the company's existence? What product or service is provided? What is the history of the organization? What is the company philosophy? How does the department in which the new employee will work contribute to the objectives of the company?

The new employee will have to know the answers to all of these questions to be able to understand how he or she "fits in."

4. Working conditions

Much of what you will want to cover in terms of working conditions should be included in the employee handbook. Don't make light of this area, however. Surprisingly enough, the majority of new employees are more anxious, initially, about such things as where to eat lunch and where to park than they are about their job description.

By clearing up some of these questions and making sure that the employee is comfortable with the "house-keeping" aspects of the job, you will be able to move on to areas that deal more directly with job performance.

You will want to let our new employee know about such things as —

- Hours of work and opportunities for flexible scheduling

- Lunch hours
- Coffee breaks
- Location of lunchroom or cafeteria
- Location of restrooms
- Company policy on personal phone calls and mail
- Payday — how often, how much, and how to keep track of this very important aspect of employment
- Special company functions and amenities such as the summer picnic, Christmas party, recognition of employees' birthdays, etc.
- Dress code
- How co-workers and supervisors should be addressed — by Mr. and Ms. or on a first-name basis

You'll be surprised at how much more relaxed your new employee will be once some of these social issues are explained. And be sure to offer plenty of opportunity for questions — there may be something you've neglected to cover that the employee considers important.

5. Job responsibilities and job standards

At this point in the orientation session you should provide the new employee with a copy of the job description for the position and go over it, point by point, so that every aspect of the job responsibilities and requirements will be fully understood.

You also want to let the employee know what the job standards are. What level of performance do you expect? How, and when, will the employee be evaluated? Be very clear about your expectations now so you can avoid problems later.

6. Company standards

You will need to provide the new employee with information on company rules and procedures. What sort of behavior do you expect from employees? How flexible is the company in terms of starting time, lunch breaks, etc.?

What are the disciplinary procedures? On what basis would a termination decision be made?

These are just a few of the areas you will need to clarify in terms of company standards.

7. Introductions

It's very difficult for anybody to remember a large number of people who they are introduced to in a short time. It's especially difficult for the new employee, who is already feeling very apprehensive about this new situation.

Your employee can be effectively introduced to the other employees of the company through a two-step process:

(a) Personally take the employee around the company to introduce him or her to the members of the employee's department and to other people the employee will work directly with.

(b) Introduce or announce the addition of the new employee through such means as a company-wide meeting, the company newsletter, etc. Encourage other employees to introduce themselves when they have an opportunity.

d. PROBLEMS TO AVOID DURING ORIENTATION

Just as in the hiring process itself, there are several problems you can run into during employee orientation. Following are six specific areas that can cause problems.

1. Telling too much at one time

A common problem encountered by many employees during orientation sessions is information overload. They are provided with too much information in too little time. There is no way that they can be expected to retain all of it. In fact, sometimes new employees will come away from the orientation session wondering if they will be able to remember *anything* they were told. This creates anxiety and can make continued training extremely difficult.

What can you do?

(a) Provide only the essentials and don't go into too much detail.

(b) Provide the same information verbally first, and then in written form as well (e.g., in an employee handbook).

(c) Watch for nonverbal cues that indicate the new employee is feeling lost, and backtrack if necessary.

You certainly can't expect your new employee to recite to you, verbatim, everything you covered during orientation. You can, however, take steps to assure that retention is as high as possible.

2. Failure to use demonstration and involvement

Teachers know that their students will learn and retain more if they are actively involved in the learning experience. Take a minute to think about it. Would it be easier to learn how to bake a cake by simply reading the recipe or by reading the recipe and actually performing the steps?

In orientation, you will be much further ahead with the new employee if you involve him or her as much as possible in the areas you cover. For instance, if you are trying to explain how the company's product is manufactured, wouldn't it be more effective to actually take the employee through the plant, pointing out the various steps in the production process as they are being performed?

Similarly, it will be much easier for the employee to understand what his or her department does by actually observing co-workers as they carry out their daily tasks.

3. Lack of patience

Most supervisors have more work to do than they can accomplish in an eight-hour day. It's not uncommon for an orientation session to be viewed as an imposition and for a supervisor to try and rush the employee through it as quickly as possible.

This is a short-sighted maneuver. Time spent now will pay off, with dividends, in the future. If you fail to cover something adequately during employee orientation, you can be sure that it will come back to haunt you later — and that you will have to spend more time clarifying and re-explaining than you would have spent if you had done it thoroughly in the first place.

4. Lack of preparation

Know what you want to accomplish and how you're going to accomplish it. Have the materials you need gathered together and organized in the sequence in which they will be presented. If you appear disorganized or confused, you will not only lose some of your credibility but you will also lose the attention of your new employee.

5. Not allowing for feedback

Don't just assume that the new employee is understanding and assimilating every fact you present. Ask. Build in chances for feedback on everything you intend to cover. Stop occasionally and ask, "Did you understand our procedure on _____ ?" Or, better yet, ask the new employee to explain in his or her own words a specific procedure or company policy you just covered.

Allow for and encourage questions. You want to do it right the first time so you don't have to redo it later.

6. Failure to reduce tension

If you fail to put your new applicant at ease, all is for naught. Review the section on establishing rapport in chapter 4 and use these same techniques in the orientation session.

After you've hired a good employee, orientation truly is the number one ingredient in assuring positive performance. Make sure you use your new resource as fully as possible. Make every step in the orientation process count!

TITLES AVAILABLE
FROM
SELF-COUNSEL PRESS

BUSINESS TITLES

ASSERTIVENESS FOR MANAGERS
Valuable advice for anyone in a supervisory position is given on effective skills for managing people. Exercises are included.

BASIC ACCOUNTING FOR THE SMALL BUSINESS
Discusses day-to-day accounting problems encountered in running a small business. Instructions for preliminary bookkeeping and organizing financial matters are given.

BE A BETTER MANAGER
From effective speaking to appraising people, to trouble shooting and to budgeting, all the required management skills and techniques are treated clearly and concisely.

BUSINESS GUIDE TO EFFECTIVE SPEAKING
A straightforward approach to developing and improving on-the-job speaking skills, with an emphasis on media techniques and the new technologies of teleconferencing and video-taping.

BUSINESS WRITING WORKBOOK
Provides exercises to practice skills that are applicable to anyone in a supervisory or management setting. Includes how to avoid writing problems, effective memos and letters, and how to write better reports.

BUYING (AND SELLING) A SMALL BUSINESS
Buying a business is often the easiest way to become an entrepreneur. This book shows how to carefully investigate the potential profitability of a business, how to assess the asking price, and how to be sure you get what you paid for.

COLLECTION TECHNIQUES
FOR THE SMALL BUSINESS
When polite reminders about overdue accounts don't bring anything but polite excuses, you don't have to give up. Here are the same successful techniques that the professionals use.

DESIGN YOUR OWN LOGO
Gives step-by-step instructions for developing an image, design-ing the logo, choosing typestyles, and refining the product; with-out the help — or cost — of a professional.

ENTREPRENEUR'S COMPLETE SELF-ASSESSMENT GUIDE
Includes comprehensive quizzes and questionnaires to deter-mine your suitability for self-employment.

EMPLOYEE/EMPLOYER GUIDE
Offers a clear explanation of labor law, including labor standards regarding age of employment, wages, hours of work, rest peri-ods, maternity leave, and much more.
Not available for all provinces and states. See order form.

EXPORTING
Details are given about what to look for in developing export markets, what pitfalls to beware of, how to deal with foreign businesses, and how to do the tons of necessary paperwork in order to export.

HOW TO ADVERTISE
This book will tell you from start to finish how to advertise your small business effectively — even if you have never done it before.
Available in Canada only.

INCORPORATION GUIDE
The practice and theory of establishing a private limited com-pany, along with the principles of limited liability are outlined and clarified. Step-by-step instructions for incorporating your company are included.
Not available for all provinces and states. See order form.

FINANCIAL CONTROL FOR THE SMALL BUSINESS
Takes you through the "after the basics" accounting procedure to show how your accounts affect your business, and how you can increase sales and success by gaining control of your books.

FRANCHISING
Buying a franchise can be a good, lower-risk way to go into business for yourself, but it is not an instant road to success. Included is comprehensive advice on identifying a suitable fran-chise and finding a good investment.

FUNDRAISING FOR NON-PROFIT GROUPS
Raising money is the most essential and also the most difficult task for any organization. This book explains how to do it, from making up the budget to approaching possible funders.

GETTING SALES
Designed to serve sales people, independent retailers, manufacturers, service businesses, and consultants, this book provides clear instructions for finding more customers and increasing sales.

GETTING STARTED
If you want to go into business for yourself, you will need to know every sales and marketing tip there is. *Getting Started* offers tips to increase sales, use effective advertising, and increase the success of your business.
Available in Canada only.

MANAGING YOUR OFFICE RECORDS AND FILES
This book outlines a step-by-step methodology for offices and organizations of any size to take charge of files and assure access to information.
Available in Canada only.

A PRACTICAL GUIDE
TO FINANCIAL MANAGEMENT
Practical advice for the non-financial manager given with guidelines on defining information needs and decision-making based on financial information.

READY-TO-USE BUSINESS FORMS
Here is a book of forms that can be torn out or photocopied as needed. It includes all the basic forms that every small business needs to make day-to-day operations easier.

START AND RUN
A PROFITABLE BEAUTY SALON
This is a comprehensive book on every aspect of operating a beauty salon. It covers everything from choosing the decor to hiring and firing staff and selling beauty products.

START AND RUN
A PROFITABLE CONSULTING BUSINESS
Gives practical information for succeeding in an intensely competitive field; from creating demand, to pricing services, to building client dependency. Sample worksheets are included.

START AND RUN
A PROFITABLE CRAFT BUSINESS
This exceptional book is for anyone who has ever considered taking up crafts, or who is already involved in crafts as a hobby, and wants to turn the hobby into a money making project.

START AND RUN
A PROFITABLE HOME TYPING BUSINESS
A home typing business is an easy, convenient way to earn good money and work when you want, where you want. This helpful guide provides all the information you need to get started and to keep your business running smoothly.

START AND RUN
A PROFITABLE RETAIL BUSINESS
Eight out of every ten restaurants fail or change hands in the first year of operation. This book is intended to prevent that. Everything from site selection to theme and menu planning is included.

START AND RUN
A PROFITABLE VIDEO STORE
The video business is booming and opening a video store is the latest way to make a fast dollar. This book guides the novice business person through the first uncertain years.

STARTING A SUCCESSFUL BUSINESS
Information regarding tax laws, purchasing an existing business, and the entire field of successful business operations is authoritatively discussed.
Editions available for Canada and U.S. West Coast only. See order form.

WORD PROCESSING HANDBOOK
This book describes the kinds of machines available and evaluates them in terms of individual businesses and their needs. It shows how to shop for the word processor you need.